Chronicles of a Walk with Christ

A WOMEN OF DIVINE ASPIRATION COLLABORATION
Copyright © 2012 by Jaime L. Rohadfox
Founder & Visionary
Women of Divine Aspiration, LLC

http://womenofdivineaspiration.org

Take note that the name satan and related names are not capitalized. The author chose not to acknowledge him, even violating grammatical rules.

CHRONICLES OF A WALK WITH CHRIST

Library of Congress-in-Publication Data
Rohadfox, Jaime L., 1966-
Chronicles of a Walk with Christ/Jaime L. Rohadfox.
ISBN 978-1-467-507-677

Cover by Lisa Brye-Sims, Graphic Designer, Chicago, Il
www.passionate2design.com

Formatting by Joy Turner, JetSet Communications & Consulting, Baltimore, MD www.joyeturner.com

Throughout All of my

Struggles

I Still Kept

my Stride

But God

Table of Contents

Preface

Women of Divine Aspiration

The vision of Chronicles of a Walk with Christ came to me at what seemed to be during the most trying time in my life – during the illness of my mother. This was a time when my fears were the strongest and my faith was at its weakest.

My mother was a God-fearing woman of immovable faith and courage. She did not believe in giving up or giving in. She did believe in me. She taught me many things, but the most important thing she ever taught me was to never give up on my dreams. I never thought the most important dream I would ever have is to have a closer walk with Christ.

My mother has gone on to be with the Lord, but it is her spirit that lives on in me and in this masterpiece that God so eloquently molded and shaped. He gave me a gift to treasure and who instilled in me the desire to know Him, intimately and completely.

I truly believe that deep in every heart is a desire to have a relationship with Christ. At some point in your life you have heard about Him, called out His name, prayed to Him, praised Him and even worshipped Him. You go to church, you read the Bible, yet there is still a void in your heart. You are not filled with the spirit of the Holy Ghost. You do not know when He is speaking to you or moving through you. You feel as though you are merely existing, lacking purpose and direction in your life.

Your life is a mess and totally out of control and you think you are not worthy enough and He couldn't possibly love a "wretch" like you. I know and understand because I along with seventeen other women, have been there. We have felt the void. We have second guessed His love for us. We, too, have felt unworthy. Yet, the one thing we also share in common is that despite it all, we had a desire for the things of God; because we are Women of Divine Aspiration.

Women of Divine Aspiration are women of Godly desire. We truly believe that if we seek Him first, He will give us the desires of our heart (Psalm 37:4). While our hearts and minds are focused on the things and the will of God, this does not mean that we are exempt from the problems of the world. However, despite the worldly influences, we have a deep desire to strengthen our relationship with Christ.

This book is a reflection of one woman's vision that transformed into seventeen women's Divine aspiration, their trials and triumphs, their walk with Christ.

These women have endured abuse, depression, lust, lack of faith, identity crisis, violence, death, grief, and witnessed some horrific events in their lives. Some walked away from Christ, only to realize that they were nothing without Him. Some weren't even trying to find Him, but He had His hand on them, nudging them to find their way into His arms.

Through this entire process, satan was all up in our Father's business. He was attempting to steal our families, kill our children's destinies and destroy our vision. God showed Himself tried and true and kept us through the midst of it all. This collaboration brought us together in fellowship, prayer and love! This collaboration strengthened our walk with Christ.

As the vessel God has chosen to facilitate this collaboration, it is my desire that you realize that your relationship with Christ is the most important relationship you will ever have. If you're relationship with Christ is non-existent, your other relationships will cease to exist. Seek Him first and He will give you the desires of your heart! Walk with us as we walk with Christ.

From my heart to yours,
Jaime L. Rohadfox

Introduction
Keep On Walkin'
Lucinda Cross

*"He told me to keep walking when approached with a challenge
He told me to walk in His footprints if I got lost
He told me to walk in love with my brothers and sisters
He told me to walk and not look back
He told me to keep my mind on Him as we walk through the valley
He told me to be patient because the last shall be first
He told me to keep on walking
...because He will never leave me nor forsake me."*

The spiritual path is not always smooth sailing. There will be difficult situations, people, gloomy days and rough times along the way. There will be moments, days, sometimes weeks when you will doubt yourself. There will be times where you will doubt the power of God and the walk you are taking with Him.

During your walk with Christ, He begins to reveal things to you. He begins to open doors for you and closes others that may harm you. You may get sick along the way. You may feel inadequate and feel like giving up. You may lose some things and people that you care about. Just know that it is part of the process. It is part of the journey that you are on when walking with Christ.

When your life is not working out the way you expect it to work, trust God, the power of God. Remember not to panic but to love and trust. Do not get distracted; but be still and walk. Do not complain or dissatisfied, but be grateful and praise Him anyway. Remember God's mercy and faithfulness. This insight will prove to be valuable, when you are walking through life with Christ rather than running through life without Him.

Many of us are too busy to walk with Christ. Some of us even start running ahead of Him. How many times have you prayed to be something, to do something, to have something, but you had too many distractions to see that the answer to your prayer was on the path that you were once walking with Christ?

I ran from God. I ran from my desire to achieve something higher and greater than myself. I forgot to breathe. Breathing is the only thing that connects you with God, the thing that you can't see, and can't live without.

When I ran from God I lost my desire for holiness, I forgot that I was supposed to keep on walking when challenges and obstacles were ahead. I forgot that I was not alone. I forgot when I was walking with my Father He was in the process of giving me an invitation to an abundant life according to Isaiah 58.

My aspiration turned into desperation. I found myself as a troubled teen, I found myself disrespectful to my parents, I found myself fornicating, lying, cheating and doing everything but walking with my Father.

I did not want to walk with Him any longer. I did not want to sing the songs that I used to sing to Him at night. I did not spend time with Him any longer. I was running from my calling. I was running from the messages He sent my way to remind me that I was a child of God.

I ran faster and farther away from my calling. I was so adamant on being the boss of my own life that I *E*ased *G*od *O*ut (EGO) and was slowly losing touch with my divine aspiration. It was easy for me to live in fear then walk by faith.

Despite all the forefathers and mothers in the bible who walked with Christ by faith like Abel, Enoch, Noah, Sarah, Abraham and Moses; I felt that faith would not show up for me. I kept on running. I was in search for Lucinda forgetting I was supposed to be searching and seeking my Father whom I ran away from. I failed to realize that my Father was with me all along.

He never left me. He was there when I was in the gutter. He was there when I was separated from my loved ones. He was there when I turned my back on Him. He was there when I became a single mom. He was there when I left my job. He was there when I left my mentally abusive relationship. He was there.

How many times have you moved ahead on your own path, in your own direction, using your own strength and leaning on your own understanding? How many times have you allowed your faith to waiver and fought fear with more fear? How many times have you looked around and God our Father was still there and all you needed to do was to keep walking?

You cannot be too busy to walk and listen to the Father. You just might miss your place in glory and your favor. Take time to walk, make time to walk.

Your walk with Christ is a personal one. Some people will try to join you and some will get left behind. Some you will feel guilty for leaving. Some challenges will fall in front of you and some at the wayside. Some may cause you to stumble, some scaring you half to death. If you stop breathing and stop walking and start to wonder and wander, doubt or fear, you will create a mountain in your path.

The journey with God is long and arduous, it is sometimes frightening and sometimes lonely, but remember God is walking with you and you are safe.

In *Chronicles of a Walk with Christ,* Jaime Rohadfox brilliantly and successfully illustrates the importance of being a woman of Divine Aspiration. Each woman's story is shared with you to relate to and grow from. Each experience is designed for you to feast on faith and fast on fear when it comes to your walk with Christ.

Jaime Rohadfox is a woman of faith who stands on Kingdom principles. She is the sister, advisor, coach, mentor, spiritual mother and leader. I know this because I have enjoyed the opportunity of being blessed by her mentorship to grow my ministry and the principles she provides have proven effective and in alignment with God's will and plan.

Chronicles of a Walk with Christ is a confirmation of God's grace. It will bless millions of women and will support them in their transition and transformation.

God knows that you learned a great deal in life and that you can help someone else with your story. God knows it's been rough and the road has been bumpy along the way. God knows that you have been hurt by loved ones. God knows that you have cried at night and sometimes during the day. God knows that you are scared.

This has not hindered these authors walk with Christ and it

shouldn't hinder yours. God knows you are seeking Him. He knows. He also knows that you are powerful, strong, and brilliant.

After reading the *Chronicles of a Walk with Christ*, let go, let God and walk. John 5:8 *"Jesus saith unto him, Rise, take up thy bed, and walk."*

In Jesus Christ name I am grateful I kept on walking with Christ, for without him I would be lost.

Beauty from Ashes

Anika N. Reese

I gave my life to Christ in March 1991. What led me to give my life to Christ was the leading of the Holy Spirit. I give honor also to my grandmother. She was a missionary. She loved the Lord first and foremost. She would take me along to church with her. Every time those doors opened, we were there. I attended church for Sunday school, worship and afternoon engagements.

Even though I was in church and in the Word, I still had many trials and tribulations. I passed them off in the flesh. I did not realize they would be a preparation for my destiny. Each trial and tribulation were designed for the work that God would later have me to do for Him.

I am in awe that I am still here! Fighting through levels of abuse – physically, emotionally and mentally, at the hands of the one who was supposed to protect me; my mother. Feeling unloved at home, I began to enter into unhealthy relationships. I was in a relationship that I thought would last forever. It ended with an unplanned pregnancy and abortion.

I spiraled into depression which ultimately led to a suicide attempt, landing me in a psychiatric hospital for four days. While there, I faced a crossroad…continue down the life of destruction or get up and get busy "living" again. The choice was to get up, finish high school and keep living. As I carried these burdens, I felt like an angel was protecting me. This was my praying grandmother! I KNOW that I know that she prayed hard for me.

On that great day in March, 1991, as the worship and bible study ended, the doors of the church were opened. The invitation was presented; this was my set up. I had a fire burning in me. I jumped up full of tears, but joyful, proceeded forward and gave my life to Christ. I had a thirst in my soul that I refused to quench, yet, could not ignore. Before I knew it, my hands were lifted high and I was presenting myself to my Abba Father!

I enjoyed attending church, reading my bible and getting to know Christ. I was ridiculed for following Christ. While many were out going to clubs, drinking, and partying, I was in church. I was a "church girl", as I was so eloquently labeled. I knew I was different, but didn't like to be treated in that way.

I never followed the crowd, especially when their attitudes and actions didn't align with my views or actions. I was taken advantage of; my kindness for a weakness. I was quiet and loved helping others. However, there was a void that wasn't fully fulfilled.

I had a yearning to be loved. I could not quite get complete fulfillment. So when others gravitated toward me, I was happy and "felt" loved. Their love was not based on what was on the inside, rather the outside. They focused on my looks, the way I walked and dressed. They did not focus on the way I communicated or that I was intelligent.

This was a hurting feeling. How could I be feeling this way when I am a child of God? I could not understand. There was a struggle between the flesh and the spirit. My flesh continued to yearn for companionship whether good, bad or indifferent.

I desired for them to focus on me and not what they could get from me. There was so much more to me than the physical. I had a strong educational background and learned from my grandmother's wisdom.

While I am still dealing with trials and tribulations; I pray and am equipped to handle them. I am continuing to seek and follow God. My relationship with my Father is the most important union!

My relationship with my Father allows me to focus on helping my children. I do understand the concept of having children within the confines of a marriage, but I did not follow that path. Not all of them were born in wedlock. While it was not God's will that they were conceived out of wedlock, He is making the best of it all!

My desire is to help my eldest child, my daughter, complete college. As I deal with my oldest son, my prodigal, I am being strengthened. I am dealing with him not wanting to move forward in life. He too is at a crossroads. Even after he physically assaulted me, I still tried to help him, because that is what mothers do. I have finally realized that the only one who can help him IS the Lord. Not me, nor a mentor, the justice system, no one but the Lord! My two younger sons are doing great and maintain positive attitudes through it all.

I want all of my children to always be evolving in life. It all begins with finishing high school, preferably with honors; and of course to attend college.

As long as my heart, mind and soul remain open, God's love will continue to penetrate my heart. The same for you applies. If you know the Word of God, it will always come back to your remembrance thus bringing about the responsibility again to follow and adhere to it.

My deepest desire from God is to remain at the center of His will and to develop an even deeper relationship with Him. As I have missed the mark, unfortunately many times, I feel that I need to make up for lost time. I want ALL that He has for me. He is the one that knows what I need, but will also provide the satisfaction of my wants as well.

I want to finish college. This desire has been put on hold since 1995, to raise my children and to work. I want to finish my bachelor's degree in Sociology and then to Law School! It is definitely within reach and the desire has never left me.

I also desire to have my household in order. I desire to strengthen my relationships with all of my children as they continue to prosper on the path that God has them to travel. I will forever be grateful to God for first forgiving me and then giving me the tools to parent.

I still desire to be married to a man that is an extension of God. He has been grooming each of us for the right time. God knows that I have been married before and I ultimately married the wrong person, because my desire was just to be married. I know that God has that "righteous" man for me and yes I will wait until He blesses me with Him.

As the Lord continues to transform me into that Proverbs 31 woman, I will continue to seek His face in prayer, study His everlasting Word and continue in relationship with Him. God is my all and all. I have not come this far on my own.

There will be many times in life when your heart may be broken. Don't give up and don't ever give in. The best is definitely yet to come! Use these times to build your courage. Your broken spirit makes you available to God.

I am thankful for each valley that I have been through, for in each was an opportunity for the Lord show Himself to me more and more. Each experience has led me more towards my vision which has created my mission...Beauty from Ashes!

Beauty from Ashes is a butterfly transforming from a caterpillar into a butterfly. There is beauty buried in ashes. I have gone through the Refiner's fire. Many overlook the ashes and the remnants of beauty still left within. One just has to sift through and then once the treasure is found, wash it off, polish it and look at it shine before the eye.

There is without any shadow of doubt that we are in a process of evolution all the time. We must be elevating as we gain more and more potential. The analogy of the life of a caterpillar shows how we must sometimes retreat or go into hibernation for a season as we face our challenges. These challenges can be generational, environmental or situational…fears, insecurities, lies that we have been told or even told ourselves; feelings of loneliness, poverty, homelessness, as some examples.

It is during the refining process that we shed the shell of those challenges that prevent us from moving forward. We leave that shell…all those burdens, curses, challenges and bask in the beauty… the beauty that has come from the ashes…the dirt…the nothing, into something beautiful and amazing in all its fullness!

As many sweep those ashes away, they never realize the treasure(s) that are buried beneath. I was glazed over, disregarded, used and thrown away. BUT, my God knew I was there and set a time for such as this to take away the pain and use to bring out the beauty and made me new. Galatians 2:20 (KJV)…*"I am crucified with Christ: nevertheless I live; yet not I, but Christ liveth in me: and the life which I now live in the flesh I live by the faith of the Son of God, who loved me, and gave himself for me."* I AM Beauty from Ashes and so are you!

I Was Mindin' My Own Business...

Reverend Barbara J. Elerby

L ike many people in a small town, I "got saved" as a teenager and faithfully went to church. As a teenager and then as a young adult, I served on the Jr. Usher Board, and sang in the choirs. I had led a sheltered life.

As a young adult, I did the typical things that young people did, hung out with friends, had my boyfriends, and even drank some. During this time, my life was easy, no real problems, no drama. I moved out of my parents' home and into my own apartment, still doing my thing, going to work, no drama. You know, *"mindin' my own business."*

After a couple of years, I moved to a big city, and life was still quiet with no major drama. Sometimes we never know how blessed we are until we hit a wall or someone enters our lives that makes us seek Jesus like never before. You know that situation which causes us to run into a local Church seeking that fresh anointing, a touch from God at His House, because the situation was just that bad.

God uses situations and/or people to get our attention when we have strayed away. I had moved, with good intentions of continuing to go to church as well as to work in the church. I could not find a church within walking distance or on a bus route, that I liked attending. Pitiful excuse wasn't it?

I ended up not going to church for several years, unless I went home to visit. Besides, Sunday was a great day to go to the show or hang out with friends… I was just *"mindin' my own business."*

But God! He had a plan. That wall I spoke of earlier, yep, I hit it. I had been experiencing wonderful work environments. I got my dream job that turned out to be the "LORD, PLEASE wake me up from this nightmare" job. I went running to church where God had His people greet me with open arms and love.

I rededicated my life to the Lord because it was only by His grace, mercy and favor that I was able to exist in this nightmare job. He reminded me that *"I will never leave your or forsake you"* (Hebrews 13:5). He showed me how to stand, after having doing all I could and to wait on Him (Ephesians 6:13). He stretched my faith when He showed me He was faithful when we are faithful. He allowed me to be a witness of His awesome power.

People asked me, "How can you work in that job, put up with the abuse and always happy, never mad." I would look at them and smile, then say "I pray and God protects me!" God used this nightmare job to bring people to Him. Praise His Holy Name!!

God gave me a new job and there were trials, but by then I was a seasoned prayer warrior. I learned how to pray and to keep my focus on Him, no matter what came against me.

I knew He had a plan for me; I just had to walk it out. It wasn't always easy; but GOD was always faithful and had me! He continued to cover me and bless me.

During this time I was injured in a car accident, which caused me to be out of work for quite a while. I started praying about my apartment and job; "Lord, my lease will be up soon, should I stay in this apartment? Should I stay in this job? Should I look to move elsewhere? Will it be this city or someplace new?"

The answer He sent me was Genesis 12:1-3, my paraphrase, *"Pack your bags and go to a land I will show you."* He was kind enough to have several Preachers preach that Scripture, over and over and over oh and just in case I missed it, over again!

I received an invitation from a friend in another city who said, "Put your stuff in storage, move here, you can stay at my house until you find a job. The job market is better here for you."

Because I can truly be one of God's *special* children, you know…

27

slow to understand His message, I didn't know if this was the area where God wanted me to move. Finally, I realized the message was truly coming from Him, so I packed my bags, made the move to this new smaller city and took my friend up on the offer.

Once I made the move, I knew I had to find a church immediately. It was during this time that I sought God like never before. I spent more time praying, reading the Bible and religious books. I did not immediately get a job; therefore, I had a lot of time to read and talk with God.

He showed me during this time that the move was about removing the distractions in my life so that He could have my undivided attention. This was a time of relationship building with God. Church was necessary; however, most important was relationship with Him. He wanted me to begin walking out my purpose for which He created me to accomplish.

Eventually I joined a church, going weekly; as *I was "mindin' my own business."* Instead it turned out to be the church where I received my call to Ministry. I began taking Ministry classes through the Church. Gone was *"mindin' my business"* and mindin' God's business.

I have faced many challenges: my lack of faith, my fear of

depending on anyone else-to include God as well as over thinking things. I used logic and would not allow my heart to be open. God used experiences such as the job and the time I was spending in church to work on these challenges with me-even removing them.

I still think things through; however, I am leaning and depending on God like never before. My faith and trust in God is so much stronger.

After a season, God called me to another denomination, where I served for a few years. He called me to my current church, where I had become an ordained Deacon, now a Reverend. I am blessed to serve under a pastor who teaches and preaches God's love. I speak of my ordination, not as bragging, but as a person who is still shocked! I mean, seriously, I was just *"mindin' my own business"* and He had a plan that He put into place for me to be all about His business.

I love working for God and for His people. I love teaching, preaching and praying for them. I am at a place of peace in Him. He has shown me that I am His unique masterpiece called for such a time as this to do His will.

I am blessed, even in the storms I am blessed because God has taught me that He has a plan and a purpose for my life, if I will seek Him with all of my heart (Jeremiah 29:11-13). He has shown me that He knew me before He placed me in my Mother's womb (Jeremiah 1:4-5).

He has shown me that I am His unique masterpiece (Ephesians 2:10); that I am fearfully and wonderfully made by Him (Psalm 139:14) for His purposes for such a time as this (Esther 4:14).

He has shown me that part of my ministry is to teach these same Scriptures from His Word to His hurting people. I am blessed more than I could ever imagine because it is all about Him. I am blessed because I am allowed to serve Him.

My deepest desire is to spread His Word wherever He sends me. I want to share The Word with the hurting people, there are so many that are in pain and do not have any idea that God is the Answer. I want all to know that even when you are *"mindin' your own business,"* God has a plan for you and He will pull you to where He needs you to do His business.

Intimacy developed through time is the key for our relationship with God. He wants us to be intimate with Him, to seek Him first in all things and at all times. We need to make time daily to be in His presence, with praise, singing, worship and prayer.

We need to "seek after Him daily like a deer pants after water." (Psalm 42:1-3) He is our "living water" (John 4:10-11); He is our answer in all things. We need to chase Him as He is our Beloved. Seek Him to know HIM (Matthew 7:7-8) and His will for your life (Jeremiah 29:11-13).

While mindin' your business, make sure you make time to be about our Father's business.

The Walk of Faith:
Operating With a Spiritual Mind Over Natural Matters

Zarien A. Daniels

Reflecting upon my spiritual journey early in life, I can truly say I had a desire to know God. During my adolescent years, I participated in the church choir, served on the usher board, as well as participated in other youth functions within the church. It was not until my early adult life that I would come to have a true knowledge of who God was as well as establishing an effective relationship with him.

Growing up in a single parent home of five siblings was very hard. Many times we went without because my mother could not provide it. We would miss out on enjoying field trips at school, or attending and participating in extra curricula activates due to the financial strain on my mother. Upon completion of high school I wanted to attend college but I knew my mother could not afford to send me. This in turn led me to join the military in order to pay for college.

It was not until I left home for military training that I realized the spiritual calling on my life. Many times when we are around our close friends and family we tend to not live up to who we are as individuals. In some instances, our personality and individuality are shaped around the thoughts and expectations of others.

I was eighteen years old when I left to attend military training. I traveled from the small town of Chattahoochee, Florida to Fort Leonard Wood, Missouri. For anyone wanting to define who they really are should consider venturing off and surrounding themselves with new people, places and things so that the real individuality of whom they are can be established.

Many of the people that attend this type of extraneous training can attest that there is a lot of stress involved. Throughout this training you are required to follow orders, team build, and complete various tactical tasks in order to be qualified as a soldier in the armed forces. I witnessed people buckling under the pressure of stress by attempting to commit suicide or requesting a discharge to return home.

It was in the military that I found my true strength in God. I have always had leadership abilities but I never knew I had spiritual leadership. I began to have prayer and bible study with other female soldiers. I shared scriptures of strength and faith for the other female soldiers to quote throughout the day to encourage them not to give up. This allowed us to cry out to God and to find hope, peace, and faith that we would make it through the duration of the training.

By the end of the training, many of the female soldiers told me how the nightly prayer and bible studies really helped them through the difficult periods of the training.

Giving God the glory, I expressed to them that I only had done what God had led me to do. From this experience, I was truly able to depend upon God's strength. My relationship with God began to evolve, giving me true knowledge of who He was in my own life.

The most difficult challenge for me within my Christian life is my Faith walk. My Faith walk is a challenge because as human beings, we have the natural instinct and tendency to react based on our emotions and how we physically feel. When we are hurt we may cry, become emotional, or depressed. If someone makes us upset we may react out of anger and may want to lash out or get even.

Think back on a time when "all hell" broke loose in your life. Or think about a time when the odds were against you and you did not see your way out. Remember when giving up was easier than holding on? It was during these times that there was a spiritual fight going on between both your "spirit and your flesh. The flesh always wants to remind us of how it can control us. Our spirit does not want us instead, keeping the faith, believing in the word of God; *Romans 8:7-8:* *"⁷Because the carnal mind is enmity against God: for it is not subject to the law of God, neither indeed can be, So then they that are in the flesh cannot please God."* *(KJV)*

This scripture is important because if you allow the "fleshly" man to work in full operation then it will ultimately result in a faith killer. The "Faith Walk" requires that you deny how you feel, praise, and shift your mindset to "God I don't know how you are going to do it, but I trust you at your word that it shall come to past." Denying how you feel is easier said than done. Trust me I know.

Sometimes the situations can be so over bearing that it is difficult to keep the faith. We become so focused on the situation, that it also becomes difficult to maintain trust in God. That is why it is very important not to focus on the situation but on the word of God and applying that specific word to your situation. Our faith in God should never be based upon what we can physically see, experience, emotionally feel, or predict as an outcome for our lives.

Our faith is tested when we can't see the expected outcome. We can apply the word of GOD in our situation and trust that he will bring it to past; *Hebrews 11:6: "But without faith it is impossible to please him: for he that cometh to God must believe that he is, and that he is a rewarder of them that diligently seek him." (KJV)*

It is not real faith until you can function within an inadequate state as if everything is perfectly okay. When you look at the definition of inadequate it means; *"Not adequate to fulfill a need or meet a requirement; insufficient."*

Without God we are nothing. We cannot fulfill our own needs, nor meet our own requirements; therefore, we are insufficient without him. We must have the real faith in God that trusts and believes that he will meet our needs according to his will.

Faith is when the devil speaks to your mind and tells you just how much he thinks you are not going to make, Yet, you instead choose to trust God with your whole heart and mind. Faith is when the doctor's give up on you but in your sickness, you trust God for your healing. It is not real faith until all hell is breaking loose in your life and you proclaim, that you have real faith in God regardless of how you may feel or what it may look like!

It is better to take your hands off the wheel and allow God to be the designated driver. Imagine yourself driving down the street; you are fully in control of the car as you have safely placed both hands on the steering wheel. Suddenly a passenger grabs hold of the wheel and you lose control of the car. This can be scary, uncertain, and a detrimental situation. This is similar to not allowing yourself to fully trust God to handle and direct the situations in your life.

When you do not trust God, you ultimately become that "passenger wheel snatcher!" Have you been there? "Here I am God I am praying, trusting and believing you for what I have asked of you in prayer but yet I have not taken my hand off the wheel because I am still worried about my situation." Can you relate? I have not taken my hand off the wheel because "I won't let the issues or the situations go within my heart."

On the other hand, maybe this is you, "Here I am with my hand in the situation trying to work out my own issue with no clear guidance from you." I admit I was a passenger wheel snatcher! I would pray but I wanted to maintain control over the situations in my life.

For most of my life I considered myself to be independent person. I rarely depended on others. This also led to me not totally depending on God. I always felt as if I could do things all on my own.

I really had to get to a place where I just let God be God. God is truly God all by himself and he does not need any help from you, me, or anyone else. When I questioned God on how I could truly let go of the wheel and allow him to lead and guide me he revealed to me his spiritual G.P.S. navigation system. God revealed to me that He was my saving grace; He was my **G.P.S**. - *G*uidance, **P**rotection and *S*trength. God will lead and guide me in the direction I should go from here on out; *Psalm 37:23: "The steps of a good man are ordered by the LORD: and he delighteth in his way." (KJV)*

God will extend his protection and grace upon me even at times when I am close to unseen dangers and God will strengthen me during periods when I am weak; *2 Corinthians 12:9: "And he said unto me, My grace is sufficient for thee: for my strength is made perfect in weakness. Most gladly therefore will I rather glory in my infirmities, that the power of Christ may rest upon me." (KJV)*

Then what is our job as Christians? We must pray, have faith, trust God at his word, and allow God to be our G.P.S. navigation system. This has to be the case regardless of how it looks or how we may feel.

I have made some significant accomplishments in my life. There are still some things that I have yet to achieve. While I have yet to be married, achieved my career goals or have begun operating within my full calling for ministry, I am convinced that GOD is just preparing me for them.

Preparing is the *"preliminary measure that serves to make ready for something; prepared for a particular purpose."* God desires that we call *those things* that be not, as *though they* were; *Romans 4:17:* *17 "As it is written, I have made thee a father of many nations, before him whom he believed, even God, who quickeneth the dead, and calleth those things which be not as though they were." (KJV)*

As it stands, I may not be married now but, God is preparing me for my husband. I may not be done with my career goals but, God is preparing me to complete my career goals, Most of all, I may not be in my full operation for ministry but, God is preparing me to walk within his true divine purpose and will for my life.

God personally knows who you are. He is just waiting for you to know who He is. God knows everything about you. He knows your faults, He knows your struggles. He knows all the tears you have shed, and all the pain you have endured.

God knew you when you were yet in your mother's wound. God will never put more on you than you can bear. You do not have to be spiritually perfect to build your relationship with GOD.

First, you have to acknowledge who Christ is in your life and accept Him as your personal savior. Secondly, confess and repent of your sins. Lastly, thrive to live a life that is holy and acceptable to Christ.

Should you fall, whatever you do, do not remain there just get back up and repeat steps 2 and 3. Without God we are nothing but through God we are everything and all things are possible through him; *Philippians 4:13 "I can do all things through Christ which strengthens me."(KJV)*

Lastly, remember to maintain a *"Spiritual Mind over the Natural Matter."* So "no matter" what it looks like in the natural & "no matter" what comes your way, you have the power to look over your situations in a SPIRITUAL MINDED way.

"I am who God say's I am and I can be who God says I can be." Be blessed in the Lord and fullness thereof. I pray peace and grace unto your life today in Jesus name, Amen.

Identity Crisis

Erin Mitchell

The year 1999 was the beginning of life; but was also a year of frustration. There was a desire in me to be loved. While it was a joyous year because of the birth of my son, it was also the beginning of a journey of finding out who I was, what I was created for and what I was here to do. It was also the year I would meet the one who created me and ultimately accepted Him as my Lord and Savior.

In June of 1997, I graduated from high school and two months after graduation, had my first son. Twenty days after the birth of my son I started college. I was a mother before I was ready, and a college student. Two years later I had two kids under the age of two.

During this time in my life I entered into motherhood thinking purpose would be found and destiny revealed. Being a teenager with two kids, I had to grow up faster to be responsible for these two lives that now counted on me for provision. My purpose was not found and my destiny was not revealed.

What began as me going to church because my friend wanted me to go with her; ended up with me giving my life to Christ. That was not my original intention and it definitely wasn't on my agenda; but God had a different plan (Proverbs 16:9).

In September of 1999, my son's father went to jail. Prior to his incarceration, we had troubles and despite those troubles, when he went to jail I felt as if a part of me went with him.

The man who gave me what I thought was my identity had just left me to raise two kids and feeling empty on the inside. I thought my self-worth was measured by the man who accepted me with two kids.

I didn't grow up in a Christian household but did go to a Catholic elementary school so I knew how to pray. One night while my two sons were sitting on the bed with me, I cried out to God and said, "Lord if you don't help me get over this man, I will never be free."

It was in that moment that I recognized that I looked at my son's father as my god. I believe God answered that prayer immediately because as Exodus 20:3 says, *"You shall have no other gods before Me."*

A few months later I went to visit a church with my friend and her boyfriend who is now her husband. The praise and worship was ok and so was the Word but I was ready to go. The service was ending and I needed to use the restroom but didn't want to get up and disrupt service.

As the pastor was ending his sermon he made the altar call for those needing to get to know Jesus. All I could think about was going to use the restroom. I was doing the dance and all and I heard him say was there was one person left to give their life to Christ.

I needed to go to the restroom or this would be an embarrassing moment for me. My mind was set on using the restroom. So the restroom became my destination. I walked toward the front of the church as if I was a puppet on the string. I had no control over my steps. While at the altar, I was wondering how did I get to the front of the church when I needed to use the restroom?

While in front of the pastor confessing Christ as my Lord and Savior; I no longer had to use the restroom and since that day the journey has been interesting, yet fulfilling.

The days, months and years after giving my life to Christ were full of hunger, zeal, passion, trials and tribulations. The one thing I still wasn't sure of was, knowing who I was. Most of my challenges in my walk with Christ were tied to having an identity crisis stemming from childhood.

I was verbally abused as a child. I constantly listened to my mother's negativity and bashing about my father who left when I was three years old. My sister would beat me up if I didn't watch her kids so she could have company. There was no family unity.

My own mother called me ugly. Although I was on the honor roll every year in elementary and junior high school and graduated as valedictorian I was called stupid. That is what I believed most of my life. I thought I was ugly so I didn't like taking pictures. I thought I was stupid so even in college I never asked questions. I thought I didn't need anyone because my mother didn't have anyone.

At twenty years of age, I accepted Christ into my life. I'm now going to church and learning about who God has called me to be in Him. I am learning that *I am fearfully and wonderfully made* (Psalm 139:14). I am learning how much He loved us (John 3:16). How could this be? I couldn't grasp any of that truth and didn't for years.

Even as the pastor and Sunday school teachers taught the Word of God, I had all the head knowledge about who God was but didn't know Him from experience. I couldn't comprehend why He loved me. I did not know how to receive His love.

There would be times I would be on a spiritual high, so full of the word after I left church. I tried to not just live a Christian life on Sundays, but every day of the week. There was still something missing; a void I thought would be filled by going to church. In the midst of trying to be spiritual I felt far away from God as the day I did before I accepted Jesus in my life.

I still did not know who I was or what I was created for and tried to walk my walk like others did. Being a very observant person, I tried to praise like others, I tried to even talk like others. I tried to fit in the church cliques, I tried to be as spiritual as others, and I tried to pray like others. I did not understand what being made in God's image and likeness meant (Genesis 1:26).

With no revelation or understanding, none of what I was mimicking was working for me. I did not know how to pray about my feelings which led me to leaving the church and God on a number of occasions.

Today, I look back over the years and unbeknownst to me, God began to reveal my identity to me in various ways. I was still blind with no revelation.

In the summer of 2011, I began to cry out to God asking, "Lord who am I? Who have you called me to be? I know you called me to the young adult ministry but what is my purpose and destiny." I wanted to know that I just wasn't a young adult leader because when that season has passed, then what?

From the day I received Christ until earlier this year, I was having a serious identity crisis. As I grew in my walk, God would give me dreams and visions but I didn't understand what they meant. Some of the dreams would reoccur over the years. There was no interpretation until as recent as the early part of 2011.

After God revealing who I was and what my purpose was, there was still doubt and uncertainty in my heart. I doubted God as a loving, faithful and patient God. He was patient with me as the blinders began to come off. I began to receive His love for me. I came to know that He loves me so much. I began to understand that He made no mistake.

Through confirmation of prophetic words, confirmation from the Holy Spirit and through His word, He has delivered me from my identity crisis. What a relief! Today I know who I am.

While still on this journey of faith pursuing purpose and destiny, it is an easier journey because there is confidence that He instilled in me that no man or devil in hell can take away from me (Proverbs 3:25-26).

I am no longer afraid of what others say about me because I know who I am. I am no longer in bondage to any man thinking my identity is tied to who he says I am. No longer do I look to any person for my value or self worth because my worth is found in

God. My confidence is in God not man (Psalm 118:8).

My journey included many ups and downs but with each one there was always a nugget of wisdom from God. One of my deepest desires from God is to know His heart and thoughts concerning His people.

As I look back and see the misery and bondage God has delivered me from, my desire is to be raised up to help set others free from the opinion of others, from the generational curses and to get to the place to know what God's purpose is for their lives.

It was frustrating to wonder what my purpose is here on earth – my true identity. I had a void in my heart that only God could fill. I am made in His image and after His likeness. As I walk by faith, my desires develop. I experience God's love in such a way that it brings tears of joy to my eyes. With each experience I have with God, I desire more of Him.

Develop an intimate relationship with God through his Word. It is in His word where He takes you on another lever in Him. It is through this intimate relationship that His will for your life is revealed (1 Corinthians 4:20).

You cannot depend on man to reveal God to you. Women have many roles and responsibilities; which demand time. You have to find time to read and meditate on the Word of God.

Once you make time to know His word, you will draw closer to Him through prayer, devotion, praise and worship (John 1:1, 4). If you don't know His word, you don't have life. If you don't have life, you don't have your true identity.

I Still Kept My Stride

Trinisa Pitts

I was about twenty-seven years old when I finally decided to give my life to Christ. Like most, I have done some things in my life that I am not proud of. Some particular things I was ashamed to talk about. However, it is the events in my past that has brought me to where I am today. I would like to take you on a journey of my life and the three D's (drugs, drinking & depression) that tried to keep me down.

My struggle started in my early twenties. I was a young parent with two children. I never missed a day of work, because money was limited. I was smoking drugs and was able to hide this for a long time until I started losing weight. I worked all day, would come home to feed my girls, put them to bed and then I would get high.

On one occasion, I went to a bar with one of my friends. This guy sat next to me. I cannot to this day remember his face. What I can remember is the conversation we had.

He asked me did I get high. I said to him no! He told me that he knew I did and that person that I am getting high with does not love me or they wouldn't be giving it to me. The rest of that night those words stuck in my head. I did not see this guy anymore that night. I truly believe that God sent this person to me to let me know that I needed to stop what I was doing.

I never told anyone about that conversation, I just went on with my life. For weeks, I continued with the same routine, working, taking care of the kids and getting high at night. One morning after getting high all night, I was getting ready for work and looked in the mirror and what I saw scared me! I saw a monster! To me it looked like the predator. Whether I was tripping or not, that day I realized I needed to stop getting high.

It was not that easy, I was in it too deep. I knew in my mind that I had to change my life but I didn't know how. I was a closet smoker. I couldn't ask for help, because I thought no one knew. I tried on my own. My drinking got heavier, trying to trade one bad habit for another.

I started to go to church; of course, this was when I didn't stay out or up late drinking and smoking. In 1998, I stopped doing drugs, but ended up with a DUI. That was an eye opener.

I realized that I couldn't do this by myself, and I needed God in my life on a consistent basis. Throughout this struggle I still had to maintain my household. I had to be the mother and the father to my girls, and give them what all other kids at their age needed. I had to learn on my own how to balance my crazy lifestyle.

I would cry all the time *"Lord there has to be a better way. I cannot live like this anymore."* God was listening to me. Things began to change in my life. February 1999 I stopped going out completely, and started to attend church regularly.

Four years later, I purchased my own home, and decided that it was time to tie up some loose ends. I decided to go back to college and complete the courses that I let go due to my drug abuse. I was working two jobs, and going to school. I was accomplishing goals, while drinking more heavily at home.

Five years later, one of my close friends I use to hang out with called me. She was having a birthday party and wanted me to come. Everyone had been asking about me, and wanted to see me. I had stopped getting high five years prior. I knew that this party would have all of my old friends there. I had to have a plan.

I called another friend who knew that I had put that part of my life in the past. I asked her to come along with me so that I could have an excuse to leave, if things got too tempting.

We attended the party and towards the end of the night my friend asked if they could leave with us after the party. I agreed, but once she walked away, I confided in my other friend that it was time to go. She said she had to go to the bathroom and I told her I would meet her at her car. I ran up the stairs of that bar and never looked back. That's when I knew I had changed.

God put me in a situation to see how I would react. He tested me to see if I was really for true deliverance. Well that was one test I passed. I knew that a momentary lapse in judgment would have undone all those years of good. When I spoke to my friend, she told me that the look on my face on that night was fear, which confirmed to her that I had to leave as soon as possible.

I conquered that demon. It was time to move on to conquer the next. It was time to work on my depression. All my life I have been a very sad person on the inside. One of the issues was not being close to my family. The other issue was not having a companion, always feeling alone.

I started focusing on God and His word. The more I fellowshipped, the stronger my faith grew. I began to feel that I was not alone and that I was loved. Despite the progress I had made, there was still something missing in my life. I needed to fill a void, but how?

I spoke with one of my former supervisors. She was a woman

of God, who told me that she would fill empty space in her life by learning new things. She told me to never stop learning and never stop taking courses. So every time I would become stagnant, I would take a course.

In August 2008 I decided to take the test to become a Notary Public. That was another great accomplishment which was attributed to the words of encouragement from my former supervisor.

I still wasn't complete. I wanted to find that peace that I felt everyone else had. There were parts of my life that just didn't seem right. I didn't know how to fix it, so I would cry. I would go out to eat by myself and look at families eating together and get teary eyed. I would look at other couples in the store or on a movie and cry. I would pray to God to send me a companion. I needed someone in my life.

The more my life changed the more I isolated myself from my friends. I had a very small circle of friends but I didn't know how they would accept the new me. I didn't know how they would accept me being a Christian, being saved.

I was initially ashamed of who I had become. I was not the person I use to be and I was scared to tell the world I had changed. I didn't know how to go around them and keep my same personality on the outside, when I knew my soul was saved.

I am a very outspoken person, so I had to learn that everyone doesn't want my opinion and don't care to hear what I think. It is very hard to recondition yourself from something that you have been doing for years. Until I could figure out how to be who I am and not be ashamed of it, I stayed to myself and started working around the clock.

Once I came home at night and I would wash off the smile I had painted on all day, and the reoccurring pain of being alone would come back. I started to talk to God even more. He was my friend and my companion all I needed was Him.

Time has passed and I am still single, and I am ok with that. I am content. The key is that I am not alone. I still do find myself crying at times, but I am sure these are tears of joy of what is to come. If God sees fit to place someone in my life, then His will be done. I was finally on a journey to find my identity and purpose in Him. I began trusting Him.

A new member of our church came to me one day after service and asked me my name. When I told her, she told me that I had a beautiful spirit. It was then that I realized that even though I was ashamed of being a child of God, it was showing up on the outside.

I had to let my light shine, and glow in Jesus name.

Today I am happier than I have ever been. I am comfortable with who I am. I am not afraid to tell the world I have been changed. Most importantly as of January 30, 2011 I was alcohol free. I did it! God did it! I would ask God to slow me down from drinking so much. What I never imagined was that He would take the taste away all together.

On September 25, 2011 I had a conversation with my oldest daughter, she said her and her sister were talking about how proud they were of me, and how much I had changed. They said they didn't understand how I could work hard all week and then drink non-stop on the weekends. She said to me that they didn't necessarily think I was an alcoholic because I wasn't hiding my drinking from them. I had to explain to her that yes I was, I was a binge drinker, a functional alcoholic.

She continued to tell me that I was very mean when I used to drink. I would get to a certain level and start calling them names and hurting their feelings. This hurt me so bad inside because I was not aware of what I was doing. I asked my daughter for forgiveness. I was a sick person then and did not know it. What she didn't know, was that she helped me to realize that I never want to be that way again.

I am now assistant secretary at my church. I was asked to take over a senior billing position after only working two years with this company. Thank God I finished taking those courses. I never would have made it to that position without that certification. What an honor for me. I am still working my part-time job, because I love it and it keeps me busy.

Last but not least I am doing something I only dreamed about since I was a kid, writing and trying to inspire others. This too is such an honor. Things are definitely changing in my life.

If you just wait on the Lord, He will see you through. I am blessed to be cleansing my body, eating healthier and losing weight safely. There is no limit to what God can do if you just believe.

One of my deepest desires from God is continued strength, hope, and the ability to be exactly what He put me on this earth to be. I have faith that He will provide. I know that He already knows there is no limit to what I will try to do.

There is something inside of me that just won't let me quit. I always push myself to the limit. I will never give up on myself or Him. *I have learned that in whatever state I am in to be content* (Philippians 4:11).

Any women on this journey and desire to know God, whatever you are trying to do, give it your all, do it to the best of your ability. No matter the consequences keep your pride, and don't lose your stride. On the outside you may look weak but God is going to make you as strong as He wants you to be on the inside.

Love yourself no matter what your past was! God can bring you out of any mess. Look at where you are now, compared to where you came from, and challenge yourself on how far you are willing to go to pursue a relationship with God. Sometimes you have to get down on your knees, pray, let go and let God.

Most importantly don't worry about those around you. Allow GOD's character to shine through your character and others will want to follow and glorify His name. Pushing yourself to the limit is the most ultimate gift you can give yourself. Find a way and get there!

My deaconess of my church and a personal friend always says "it is personal." I never really understood what she meant until I started my journey. Your walk with Christ is a personal one. It's between you and Him.

I am hoping that if you are struggling to conquer the three D's (drugs, drinking & depression) in your life as I had to in mine; you will see that giving up is not an option. I worked harder and smarter to accomplish my goals and you can do the same.

Whenever you feel like you are running energy, and don't know which way to turn; just close your eyes and repeat "*I can do all things through Christ who strengthens me*" (Philippians 4:13). Whatever you do, *just keep your stride.*

May God bless and keep you underneath his wings.

Under Construction

Minister Kathy Hodge-Davis

Mommy, I am going to join church tomorrow." At the tender of age of 12 I spoke those words to my mother. It was after all, the time that every good girl should give her life to Christ. It was tradition.

It was my mother's smile as I spoke those words that make this memory a very vivid one. It has been forever etched in my memory bank as the beginning of a new journey. It was the beginning of a road that would be long and hard some days, tiresome others, just pure joy many days exhausting.

Since that day I have tried to do all the things a "Good Christian" ought to. I sang in the choir, served on the usher board, attended conferences, joined ministries, served in a variety of leadership roles for different auxiliaries, and have even been the worship leader. I remember one day thinking to myself "If this is what it's like to serve God, then I've got it made." I really had no clue.

One day I met a woman who said point blank. *"You know all the right things to say and all the right things to do. You have head knowledge of Christ. But, do you have a real relationship with Him?"* I was taken aback to say the least. As I began to think about it, that wasn't the first time I had heard that. This time, however, there was something different about those words.

This woman had a fire and a desire that seemed to permeate her very being. Her closeness to a Holy God was so overwhelming and so enticing that just being in her presence was a real encounter with Christ. I knew then that I wanted, NO, I needed to have that same connectedness to Christ. I became a stalker, if you will, and I began what I now call a *"Hot pursuit of Christ in my life."*

My pursuit of Christ began at age twelve but it wasn't until the age of thirty-seven yes, some twenty-five years later that I would fully come to know who I was and who I am in Christ.

It would not be one defining moment but many encounters with Christ and His faithfulness that brought me to Him. Encounters like the agonizing pain I felt watching my sick child lay in bed with a tube stuck in his little swollen hand at the age of four. He stayed in that hospital room for seven days.

One day five preachers from a nearby church came and laid hands on my son and prayed for him. On day six my son was dancing in bed; on the seventh day my son was released. My faith was tested during this time. I was not ready but God was preparing me. It would be the beginning of a prayer life that has been fruitful ever since.

Looking back, my life was *"under construction"* and I did not know it yet. I thought I knew Christ but each new day brought me closer to Him. It was a burning flame, a fire that refused to go out.

At that point, more than ever, I felt ready to do all I could to keep that fire burning. But, life happens and sometimes where there should have been a flame there was a flicker. When I should have prayed more I found it difficult to pray at all. When I should have served more I found it hard to serve at all. What was the problem you may be asking? The problem was me. I was my own challenge. God was calling me to serve and I was running.

In the beginning I was like the race car driver heading for the finish line looking for the checkered flag to signal a win only to find the yellow flag to signal a warning. It was a warning that I was headed for trouble. This walk with Christ is not by any means an easy one but the challenges in my walk were me not anyone or anything else, simply me.

When people told me that they believed God had a calling on my life, I did everything I could to sabotage that calling. When I spoke words of comfort through God's word to others, they recognized this calling. When they told me, I became silent.

I taught Sunday school and when five children joined the church from my class, I stopped teaching. I stopped singing in the choir, I even stopped going to church. I would do whatever I needed to do so that God could not use me.

My daughter became sick in her junior year in college. It was an illness that left her in much pain. We took her to the doctor. They prescribed some medicine and we sent her back to college. An overdose of medicine left her hospitalized for fourteen days.

The doctor told my daughter that she had to have a relationship with Christ because there was no way she should have been living with all of the medication she had in her system. That statement and seeing her in the hospital for so long left me afraid to open my mouth to God. I could not understand what I had done that would cause Him to punish my child. So, I spoke no words at all.

I was paralyzed in fear and it took more than a year to fully recover. Depression grabbed hold of me and kept me in a stronghold for more than two years. My pastor said my influence and affect on the people had changed. He had no idea my whole life had changed. I found myself taking medication for depression as if it was my best friend. I went through life as if it did not exist.

My daughter recovered, graduated twice received her bachelor and master degree. My son was well, but I was still struggling. My children had found healing from God, but I was still struggling, I was still running. I had lost my passion for being close to God because of fear.

Fear led me to a life of disobedience. Because of that disobedience, I have suffered bankruptcy, foreclosure, repossession and a broken heart.

Fear had such a strong hold on me that it clouded my judgment and caused me to willingly throw away my desire to be close to God. I often asked myself during this time of struggle *"What happened to the passion, the desire, the "Hot Pursuit?"* How could I have drawn so close to God, yet, be so willing to throw away that relationship?

I was an oxymoron to myself. I loved the Lord, but not that much? It was a constant battle. I guess I hadn't heard that the battle wasn't mine, but that it battle belonged to the Lord. I guess that I had not heard that now that I had found God, the struggle was over.

Once I got out of my own way I came to understand that the revelation was already in the invitation. God had already designed His purpose, His plan, and His goals for my life. I just needed to trust Him.

Once I accepted that Christ was already working on my behalf, I could see the manifestations of His goodness in my life. God had worked it out. How did He work it out? I accepted my calling and in 2009 was licensed into Ministry.

I began this journey kicking, screaming, and crying. Those things eventually turned into praying, worshiping and praising. Today, I am destined in Christ. I stopped majoring in the minor things of life. Those minor things are: the opinions of others, those who do not understand my calling, those who don't like the church I attend, and those who don't like the way I praise or worship.

All that is really minor compared to a major occurrence some 2000 years ago when Christ died for my sins. Today, I understand that after the shout, after the dance, that getting back to the basics is where I am.

The basics are: fasting, praying, and praising. These things have led to a *"Rock that is higher than I"* (Psalm 61:2).

What I desire from Christ is not something for myself. Yes, I want more of Him. Yes, I desire to know Him more intimately but my deepest desire is that, *"His name be declared in all the Earth"* (Exodus 9:16). I want all to come to know Him as "Adonai", "My

Lord," "I am that I am", "The Lord God", "The Lord our Father." It's not about me.

In my forty plus years of life, I was in "hot pursuit," "running with no place to hide," "in a state of fear," and finally, opening my heart."

In my journey I have learned that when I open my heart to Christ and to the things of Christ I experience love, joy, peace, and contentment. Sometimes I experience sadness, and sorrow but I don't have to stay there because even in the midst of trouble, Christ is a very present help.

Today, I've come to realize that He has called me and positioned me to do the work. And I am just like my sister Esther, *"If I perish let me perish"* (Esther 4:16).

God is doing something new in my life each day and He will do the same thing for you. He has kept you alive through the struggles and brought you to the Kingdom, *"for such a time as this…"* (Esther 4:14).

Whiter Than Snow

Daphne Tarango

I was born into a Christian family. I'm a preacher's kid and a preacher's grandkid. I've been in church all my life, and you would think I would have had it all together by now. But that is furthest from the truth.

In 2009, as I entered my thirties, I longed to get closer to God, to know what He wanted for my life, and to do it. In my quiet times, I was feeling that I needed to confess. All I could think of for weeks was the hymn, *"whiter than snow."*

On Sunday, April 5, 2009, I confessed I had done all the "right" things in my Christian life but one. For thirty-three years, I struggled with whether I was truly saved. I've always been in church. I had gone through seasons of certainty, where I said, "Yep, I'm good" to seasons of uncertainty, "I'm not so sure." Every time, I rationalized it away.

On that Sunday, April 5th, I admitted I was not 100% certain I was saved. This troubled me more than it ever has, especially given all the growth and freedom I had experienced the previous five years

73

after my divorce. Regardless, I did not want to continue with this inner turmoil any longer. I wanted to be certain. I wanted to have the assurance and the memory that I had truly accepted Jesus Christ as my Lord and Savior.

On that Sunday afternoon, I realized that through all my life struggles, I had come to love God so much that it grieved my heart to even consider the possibility that He could look at me at the end of my days and say, "I don't know you." That thought alone was enough for me to take the biggest step in my recovery. I ignored all of the self-criticism in those moments and the "What would people say?" Once and for all, I did it. I prayed to receive Jesus as my Lord and Savior – at the age of thirty-three, with one of my dear friends by my side. I am now 100% certain that I will spend eternity with the lover of my soul.

I cannot explain the events of my life, but I believe that from the moment I was born again on April 5th, 2009. God had been wooing me with his grace, a sinner. On that day, I was finally at a place where I had come to love Him more than anything. Swallowing my pride and making it official, no matter how foolish it might appear as a preacher's kid, was my way of showing Him.

I wasn't always free. My low self-worth imprisoned me for most of my life. From childhood, my family and I spent a lot of time together. If my brother and I weren't at school, we were at church, or at activities like girl scouts or little league baseball.

My parents took us everywhere they went, even to work sometimes. I loved spending time with them. Two of my favorite memories were going fishing and eating smoked mullet while we waited for the fish to bite and getting ice cream at a corner ice cream shop in the city where we lived. I can still taste the upside down banana splits.

Although we spent a lot of time together, I didn't feel like anyone really knew me. I don't remember ever talking to anyone about what I liked, didn't like, what I was feeling, my dreams, my hurts. My family didn't discourage us from expressing ourselves, but neither did they encourage it.

I love my parents dearly, and they did the best they could with the skills they had. But they didn't know me. I didn't know them. I didn't know myself. I didn't know how I could be loved the way I longed to be loved. I felt too dark around lighter-skinned relatives, so I believed I could not be loved for who I was.

At age five, a babysitter introduced me to soap operas, where I learned I could do things to be loved. So I imitated what I saw. From childhood, my life was consumed with performing and striving. As a teen, I absorbed everything I read and saw in soap operas, teen versions of romance novels, and teen magazines.

I craved perfection. I couldn't mess up. What would people say? What would God say? I just needed to try harder. But it wasn't enough; I was not enough. I judged everything I thought, said, or did harshly, getting mad at myself and obsessing over the smallest details. I wanted to prove myself; instead, anger sprouted within me.

I married at age twenty. We had our difficulties, just like any marriage. We had happy moments, but for me, that's all they were - moments. I just couldn't seem to ever get myself to a happy place and stay there for an extended period of time. Our conversations centered on the weather, work, school, TV shows, music, other people. We were more like roommates, and it angered me even more.

My striving continued. most days. I worked from the time I woke up to the time I went to bed. I had a brilliant career ahead of me, and I was proud of my achievements. I was very close to finishing my PhD. Still, I was empty. I desperately wanted more out of life, but my career was the only thing I could control; it gave me my worth. I held on, even though I was irritable, critical, sarcastic, and depressed on the inside. Outside, I wore a smile.

When I felt most alone, I would write. As I put my thoughts and feelings on paper as best I could, my heart was free – even for a few moments. We started to attend church regularly, and I learned about having a personal relationship with God – not based on performance or rules. What a breath of fresh air! I prayed and read the Bible--things I knew a Christian should do, but I resisted transferring control of my life to God.

In early 2004, my husband asked for a divorce. I begged and pleaded, "Please, no. Let's get help." But he didn't want to try anymore. I felt like he was giving up on me, that I was a hopeless cause, and I would never change. My life took a sudden turn. I attended church alone. I despised my attitude, and I desperately wanted to be a different person, but I didn't know how to change. I was critical of others because I was critical of myself.

I wanted to measure up and make all things right--to be a better wife. I read all the self-help books I could find. I ventured into online pornography, and before I knew it, I was addicted. I couldn't stop.

My divorce was final in 2005--eleven years of my life dissolved in seven minutes in a courtroom. The rest of the year piled on more hurts. I kept doing the same things and expecting a different outcome. I entered into unhealthy relationships. There were broken family relationships. I began falling behind on my Ph.D.

I longed to make at least one thing work. Instead, my body caved under the multiple stressors. Doctors and counselors encouraged me to reinvent my life. Deep down, I knew I wanted to do one thing, resign my PhD. As I ended that chapter of my life, questions echoed through my mind: "Daphne, what will they say?" But in my heart, I felt relief.

I didn't know what to do with my life, but I wanted a fresh start. Within a month-and-a-half, I had a job and a home church in sunny Florida. I was now ready to change. But change doesn't come easy.

God started the recovery process with my addiction to work. He helped me to set boundaries on my work day and to resist the urges to do a little more, to overanalyze, and to sit at the computer just a little longer. I couldn't do that on my own for years! God then cancelled the effects of pornography, soap operas, and romance novels. The moment I threw them out of my house, I was free. I have set boundaries on what I watch and listen so I don't fall back into that trap.

Other issues have been more difficult for me to overcome, such as rescuing and fixing people, approval addiction, people pleasing - saying yes when I wanted to say "No," prioritizing the needs of others over my needs; keeping silent instead of speaking up; compromising my values, so that others would like me, and becoming a venting ground for others to dump their problems on me.

I mistook all of these things for acceptance and intimacy. They were counterfeits! I was still empty, and my body was caving again.

I needed help, so I started Christian counseling. In the very first session, I came out of denial. I am codependent: I am addicted to controlling people, behaviors, and things to try to control my inner feelings of low self-worth.

After that first counseling session, I searched for scriptures about how God truly felt about me. Slowly, I started to believe that I did matter to God. I learned that God loved me for me, not what I what or wouldn't do. He loved me before I ever did a single thing (Titus 3:4-5). And He has known me from the very beginning (Psalm 139:13).

He knows my innermost desires, my hurts, and my struggles. Even when I can't put words together to tell Him how I feel, He understands the cries of my heart (Romans 8:26). No one knows me like He does. I don't need to strive with Him. I can just be–and He won't ever stop loving me (Jeremiah 31:3). He won't ever reject me. Yes, I still struggle, but believing truth always sets me free.

Several months after I started counseling, I wanted to help others experience the healing I was now experiencing myself. I became a leader in a Bible-based 12-step recovery program at my church. All leaders were required to take the 12 steps for themselves. What a breakthrough! I have never known such safety and intimacy.

Others knew my secrets but never held anything against me, judged me, or treated me any differently. They loved me unconditionally. Freedom in Jesus Christ has forever changed my life--only for the better.

As a recovering people-pleaser, it has been difficult for me to set boundaries in unhealthy relationships and if necessary, end them. Some people in my life have been quick to accept my new boundaries. There were times when my own family was not happy. Eventually, they began to come around. We now have a better relationship than I've ever known.

My mom and I are more than just mother and daughter. We are friends. I wouldn't trade my relationship with her for anything. My dad has made so much progress of his own. He calls me sometimes out of the blue to tell me he loves me and he's proud of me. Yes, we still have our conflicts, like any family, but I chose to forgive and to love them. My brother and I do not have much of a relationship. But

I hold on to hope.

There are others have not accepted my healthy boundaries, and it is still very difficult for me to let them go. Mostly, I miss the familiarity of these toxic relationships. But every time, I know I have done the right thing.

Making amends to people I have wronged has and continues to be one of the biggest positive changes in my life. Confessing to others regularly and just saying, "I'm sorry. I was wrong" has been life-changing. When others haven't accepted my attempts to make amends, I know I've done my part, my conscience is clean, and their response is theirs to own--not mine.

Day by day, God is breaking my chains. I can now say, "No" without feeling guilty. I feel the need to rescue or to save others. I give of myself because I want to not because I feel obligated to. I am more able to share my feelings in a healthy way, without fear of rejection. These are big deals for recovering codependents! I'm not cured, but I celebrate these and other small victories.

When I slack off and get too comfortable, I relapse into my unhealthy habits. Praying and meditating on God's Word helps me to stay close to Him.

He has identified other areas I have needed to surrender to Him, including fear, food addictions, anger from my recent struggles with chronic illnesses, and post-traumatic stress disorder.

In mid-2009, I was diagnosed as having bipolar depression disorder. I now understand how my illness has played a part in my mental, emotional, social, and physical health. All of my experiences have helped me to accept that it's okay to get help-- from family, friends, counselors, doctors, recovery groups, and yes, even medications.

Today, I stand in freedom because God has had my hand in His the entire time and through all these experiences. He alone has brought me out step by step with His unfailing love.

My desire is to comfort hurting people with the comfort God has given me (2 Corinthians 1:3-4). As I glorify Him in all I do, He keeps opening doors for me to share my story and experiences with others--face-to-face and through my writing.

Dear one, I am whiter than snow. God does have a plan and a future for me (Jeremiah 29:11), and He is working everything out for my good (Romans 8:28).

In 2010, He brought my Prince into my life--although I did not know it at the time. God's timing was perfect--not only for me but also for the man who is now my husband. He is God's gift to me. He is a man of leadership and servant hood. He is a man of strength and tenderness. He is a man of love and faithfulness. He is a man of God.

I thank God for His cleansing power. I am *whiter than snow!* Daily, I celebrate my freedom in Christ. He continues to set me free, and I, in turn want to offer you hope that you too can be free from your prison, to the glory of God the Father.

Dear one, you can be *whiter than snow!*

Faithful to the Call
Sylvia White

As far as can remember I was different from most of my family, I called it many things but as I grew and mature I realized that it was the call of God on my life.

I received Jesus into my life at eleven years old and one year later I received the Holy Spirit with the evidence of speaking in tongues. I was invited to church by some children at school. I saw them walking to church every Sunday morning and afternoon. They always looked excited and like they were having so much fun.

I asked my mom if I can go and she said yes! My life would change a few months later during a "back to school" revival. It became something greater than I could ever imagine. I saw my life in a new state. I had a hope that just was so strong for me, it all began to make sense, and I was now comfortable in my soul.

As time went on, things got tougher. I was in a Baptist home trying to live a Pentecostal life style, but I had peace. The enemy began to fight me on every side. I was only thirteen years old. He knew what was getting ready to happen in my family. If he could just get me to renounce this peace in my life, he could stop the revelation of the Word of God from happening in my family.

I stood firmer than I had stood before. I remained faithful to this new commitment in my life. Later my family began to see the real change. They began to receive Jesus as their personal savior. God had used me; this pre-teen to bring the revelation of a real relationship with Christ to my family. That was only the beginning of the manifestation of the call on my life.

As time went on I was drawn toward children. I saw what God did with me and realized that if other children received Christ as their personal Savior they could change families all over this world. I realized that this change could happen, but I would not accept this mandate on my life until years later. I did stay faithful to minister to children.

Opposition was hard for me to understand in the church because I thought being saved meant I would finally experience peace. I didn't realize it had to be maintained with the Word of God.

I became relaxed and was involved in a relationship that ended and brought a lot of pain that I thought I couldn't bear. I was sixteen years old when it did end. It took many years to be healed from it and to realize this was not God's best for my life.

The break up landed me into a relationship that satan thought would end my life. But God was still protecting me in the midst of my disobedience. I married at the age of twenty-two. My life was in a world spin for the next twelve years. I was in depression from my first year of marriage. I was wondering if God could still hear me and why He was allowing me to go through all of this pain. These were my dark years.

I did not lose hope in Him and His ability to deliver me. Yes, I was in church every time the doors opened. Yes, I was praying, but was He hearing me or was He just watching? During this same period of time I had three pregnancies and one miscarriage that I dealt with alone.

I had a dream that I was at another church and I saw the building so clearly. The next morning I went to look for this building and I found it. I went in and it was a revelation of the Word that I never heard before. The pastor talked about faith and he was teaching with such an anointing.

I left the church where I first received my salvation and joined this one. I began to apply what I was learning to my life, the depression was lifting but it wasn't gone. One day it got to a point where I thought, it was just not worth it anymore. The spirit of depression intensified its hold on my life.

I went to church that night to say goodbye and told everyone how much I loved and appreciated them. BUT GOD! He had a better plan that satan could not stop. Before the service ended and in the middle of the benediction the Lord spoke to the pastor and told him someone in the congregation was going home to end their life. The pastor spoke against the spirit of depression and commanded it to be loosed off of their life. Immediately it was loosed. I was free!

I heard the Lord clearly speak to me at that point. He told me to go to Isaiah 62: 1-2 and read it three times a day. He revealed to me if I was obedient, I would totally be delivered and I would never have to fight that spirit again.

I never had to fight it again because of God's deliverance the war was over! Just like someone who is delivered from alcohol, they stop going to bars and having alcohol in their homes.

I began to monitor what I watched, listened to and what I did very carefully. I did a lot of laughing. I got out of that marriage. I began to realize hope again and that God had a serious plan for my life. He brought back to remembrance that He had called me to minister to children and their families. I had a mandate that must be fulfilled. He revealed to me that there were children that were waiting on the love that God has equipped me with to give to them.

I accepted that call more and more. I began to dream again. The dark years were over and God had come through like He always said He would.

I am now happily married and God has moved us to a church in Goose Creek, SC where we have been members for thirteen years.

My new husband and I are serving as children coordinators. I have written a book "The Heart of Faithfulness", and I am the producer of "All About the Kingdom Kids" a local cable show.

Even after this level of achievement I still desire to have a closer relationship with God and most importantly fulfill His call on my life with diligence and excellence.

I am asking God to show me daily how to make a difference in a child's life. I am asking Him to reveal to me the families I can talk to about making Him the center of their life. I want to know how to display his love each day.

Life only ends when you give it the okay to end. God has called each of us to do something in the earth. God has called us to touch lives that only we can touch with the gift that He has given us.

Yes, there will be many distractions along the way but the wonderful thing is in Psalms 97:10 the Lord tells us how *"He guards the lives of His faithful ones.*" He watches over those who are faithful.

He walks in the calling that He has placed on our lives. Be diligent and faithful to your calling and watch God show out in your life as you touch the lives of others.

Let's Make a Deal

Effie Alofoje-Carr

I made the deal of a lifetime sitting in my car one hot summer day in 2004. It started earlier that year during my senior year of high school. I talked to God everyday on the drive to school and I just knew He was listening.

My mother instructed me to pray when I got in the car since I was a new driver. Well, I actually followed her instructions. I would talk to God every morning. Often I shared that I felt there was more to Him than what I knew or experienced.

I was raised Catholic, but at a young age I had developed a desire to be intimate with Him, I just never knew what that meant or felt like. At age eleven, I requested my baptism because I wanted God to be in my life and deep down I sensed His presence.

I was not taught He wanted a personal relationship with me. By age seventeen, I began seeking Him about there being more to Him than what I knew, I had no idea the journey I was on would lead me straight to the cross.

I continued to talk with God daily. Despite my growing prayer life, my senior year was difficult. One day, it became too much to handle. I sat in a corner and cried uncontrollably for hours. A close friend had the same experience that day, so together we sought the advice of a trusted security guard whom we loved.

She spoke to us about salvation, and how she came to find Jesus Christ. She instructed us to get down on our knees and pray and give our lives over to Christ. I did exactly that, but I did not really feel much change. She had planted a seed of faith that inspired a close relationship with God that was growing in my heart.

I failed a math class that resulted in my diploma being held, so I did not graduate on time. I had to pass the class in summer school. I had already been accepted into my school of choice for college.

If you could only imagine how not having a high school diploma would ruin my college plans completely. I believe this was a significant event in my life that caused me to seek God in a way I never had before. Boy did I find Him!

I was casually "involved" with a guy, who significantly added to the chaos and difficulty of that year. He called me the day I got home from college orientation. His news was grim. His admission to the same school I was attending had been revoked. I was terrified. He graduated...on time...and passed the class I failed. I was dead meat for sure. "Lord, get me out of this!" I cried.

I sat in my car in front of my parents' house and that day I made a promise to God that I am willingly keeping to this very day. I said "God, if you get me through this and get me there, I'll serve You. I'll do whatever You want. Just get me to college."

I had no idea what I was getting into! He definitely answered my prayers. I know without a shadow of a doubt I should have failed that summer class, but I didn't.

The college received my transcripts even though they should not have been sent without me graduating. There were no questions asked. I got a welcome letter, a dormitory address and a hefty bill in the mail.

Although I had stopped attending Catholic services and worked at my retail job Sundays, I faithfully listened to gospel music and discussions on the radio until I left for school. I learned about Divine favor. This was truly it!

After leaving for school I had no idea what was waiting ahead for me. I was just grateful to be on the path to what I thought was success by obtaining a college degree.

God answered my prayers, and although I did not forget my promise to serve Him, it was not a guiding precept. The actual work of salvation was not in my plans because I did not know what the lifestyle entailed at the time.

Immediately after starting college, I was drawn to the gospel choir on campus. I started attending rehearsals regularly. Gradually I attended the Apostolic campus Bible study affiliated with the choir.

After my initial church visit I refused to go back. I was uncomfortable at the church because it was spirit filled, but choir and Bible study were not in my opinion.

I grew quickly and was baptized in the Holy Spirit without any guidance. I'm sure somewhere in that time period I "officially" gave my life to Him, I just do not recall the exact moment.

Armed with what I knew to be salvation, I did not expect to struggle, rather to remain pure and righteous. There were many times in my walk where I was heavy laden, carrying the burden of my sins.

Despite the heaviness, I never turned my back on God. I never stopped believing Him, I never stopped serving Him. I did not miss church often. I was always terrified of condemnation for my sins.

I struggled to have faith in God's word that He would complete the good work He began in me. I was convinced my sins were too much and God could never "fix" me without a little help from none other than myself of course!

I constantly made decisions in an effort to rectify my sins. Silly of me to think God was logical, practical and cut and dry like I had a tendency to be.

Love covers a multitude of sins, not rituals, beliefs or behaviors to "fix" the sins! None of us are immune to challenges. Most of us will see rough spots in marriage, finances, maintaining good friendships, staying healthy, in our families, trying to fulfill a goal (such as weight loss or education) and other cares of life at any given season.

Over the years I endured many challenges in all of those areas. Some were attacks from the enemy. Some were self-inflicted as a result of my efforts to bandage my sin.

I had serious financial troubles, struggling to keep a stable home. There was strife in my marriage when I made choices I believed would "fix" my sins. The challenges in my health were the attacks of the enemy. God revealed to me that these challenges and struggles were allowed for His divine purpose and to get the glory.

In the beginning of our marriage, my husband and I we were blessed to join an amazing church and gained the most extraordinary spiritual parents. Our connection to the ministry led us to make the tough decision to be unified as a couple at very low points in our relationship. We decided to stick it out just one more day.

The genuine love and support of our pastor and his wife gave us more hope than we initially dared to have. We came to them badly broken from a ministry that hurt us deeply.

The leader attempted to destroy our character. Church hurt can be the worst hurt because most of us expect the best from God's people. This is why it's better to put your trust in God than in man.

When you are faced with obstacles in ministry, remember the church is made up of the very people God sent His Son to die for on the cross. Although those years of intense struggle were pretty painful and lonely, they were not in vain.

Today, my primary battle is living a balanced, healthy lifestyle. I have made peace with some of my most difficult trials, one of which was finishing my degree. I had major financial setbacks and I also found myself on academic probation, facing expulsion.

For almost two years I could not afford to enroll in classes, but when I returned, I was released from extended probation. I made the dean's list and finished my degree within a eighteen months.

Today I have a stable household, flourishing marriage, my bachelor's degree, friends I can trust, and church leaders that are trustworthy and love us as their children in a dynamic church ministry.

Nothing is perfect, but I have seen God's healing power work in my life and in those closest to me. There are difficult times because people are people. Fortunately my outlook has changed and that makes all the difference in how I handle challenges.

My deepest desire from God is to become the woman of my dreams. I desire to become that woman who intentionally creates a fabulous life, the best life possible and teaches other women how to do the same.

I believe we can have it all once we give our lives to Christ! God has called us to have heart stirring marriages. He desires for us to enjoy and have fulfillment in the work we do. He wants us to have delightful children and home lives. He instructs us to reach those far from Him with authenticity and love.

He's called us to be in good health and prosper. He wants us to enjoy the life He's given us and overcome the challenges of life by using our renewed minds in Christ.

I am excited about building a beautiful life and helping women everywhere do the same. In order to make that happen, it takes much prayer, diligent studying of His Word, reading good books, a strong work ethic, building strong relationships, allowing exposure to bigger and sometimes intimidating things and people, a teachable spirit, and radical, unshakable, unmovable faith.

As I continue to progress, God calls me to change in ways that make room for His promises to manifest. I'm working to create more order and organization, so I can be prepared when we finally have our own home.

I fight harder to guard my mouth and speak life over situations and people since the power of life and death are in our tongue. I'm working to maintain a consistent image that fits my style profile. These are just a few areas the Holy Spirit has convicted me in to prepare me for my destiny. I have made changes in my faith. I have better stewardship over my time, finances, and body to create an atmosphere that removes self-imposed limitations and gives freedom for God to move in my life and fulfill the desires He's placed in my heart.

I am a twenty something year old female from the inner city who expects greater things are still to come. I encourage you to raise your expectations of God and life and be crazy grateful for just who you are and what you have.

No matter where you are right now, God is trying to draw you closer Him. He wants to give you more. Even if you are in a difficult season, there are so many great things happening around you if you change your perspective and have a grateful spirit.

Acknowledging these good things causes a shift in your expectations and gives God a reason to give you more. It is not always easy. As a matter of fact it is usually pretty difficult. The results are well worth it in the end!

In faith I made a deal with God and He was faithful beyond what I even asked, and never once have I regretted following Him. I now understand everything that happened was His way of leading me and drawing me into His presence.

He desires to answer your call. He will give you something greater than you ever imagined. If you are grateful, obedient and expecting it with great faith, He will show up!

Hebrews 11:6 tells us *"But without faith it is impossible to please him: for he that cometh to God must believe that he is and that he is a rewarder of them that diligently seek Him."*

Declare this today:

Lord, let's make a deal. You'll lead and I'll follow. I believe your son Jesus died for me and that seals this deal. From today forward I will believe whatever is true, whatever is noble, whatever is right, whatever is pure, whatever is lovely, and whatever is admirable. I will surrender my life to you and your plans for me, plans to prosper me, give me a hope and expected end. I will live my life for You and Your plans for me...well they'll blow my mind. You will show me open heavens, miraculous life changes and a permanent shift of my mindset. No matter what, You never change, Your Word is unchanging and even if I don't always follow, don't always believe, I have faith You will show goodness and mercy and guide me back to You.

He's leading you to Him. Respond in faith. Girl, put on those sneakers and start running!

102

Learning to Walk Through the Hurt

Tracey L. Massey

I gave my life to Christ in February of 2001. The day I joined the church was also the day they were holding a Baptism service. This particular church held Baptism services sporadically throughout the year.

By God's Divine plan, I was saved, baptized, and filled with the Holy Spirit all on the same day. Yet, I had no idea what any of this meant or what lied ahead for my life. My head was spinning.

I did not have the "luxury" of growing up in church. I did not know "church protocol." What I was being taught and what I was living were totally different. My heart ached and I did not know why.

Wanting to be who God said I was and remaining the same, would become a struggle that I would have to grow through for a long time.

The day I gave my life to Christ, I felt like a huge burden had been lifted from my shoulders. I knew that things would never be the same. I was a new person with a new beginning.

My heart raced and I had this feeling of peace overtake me. I did not feel deserving of this love. All I could think about was the mess I had made of my life. I did not understand how someone could love me in spite of me. I did not understand how someone would want me deformed and not good enough.

"Damn! I'm still here." These were the words that came out of my mouth when I woke up alone in a hotel room after trying to commit suicide. I had taken enough pills to bring a grown man to his knees. I had lost all hope, but I woke up.

The night before, my five year relationship had ended with the man whom I thought would one day be my husband. Was he the reason why I wanted to end my life? No. It was the culmination of all of the events of my life. The breakup was just the icing on the cake.

It did not matter that I had a daughter who needed me. It did not matter that I had friends and family who loved me and wanted me to have the best. I was broken.

My mother had died after a long illness. I had lost a child due to an ectopic pregnancy. My boyfriend and I made the toughest decision to have an abortion after finding out I was pregnant again. It was one thing after another and the weight was too heavy. No one seemed to see the pain I was experiencing.

As I sat on the edge of the bed in my room, I remember the tears rolling down my face. I could not stop crying. Then…it happened. I heard a voice say, "If you try this again, you will be a vegetable for the rest of your life. I am not done with you. I have work for you to do."

I looked around the room even though I knew there was no one else with me. At that moment, this overwhelming warmth came over my body. There was a void in my heart and I knew that it could not be filled by anyone.

I remembered a friend of mine telling me about the church she attended. She invited me to visit. I knew I had to get to that church. She gave me directions to the service. Oddly enough, she was not in attendance the day I decided to go.

It seemed as though God had strategically placed each person in my path as I walked into the church. Every song, prayer, Scripture, and greeting tugged at my heart with such a strong pull that I could not contain my tears.

There were people who had tried to convince me that there was more to life than what I was living. I remembered all of the people who prayed for me after my mother passed. I realized that all of those people had planted seeds in my life. The day that I gave my life to Christ was the day that those seeds were being watered. From that day on, I knew everything was going to be ok.

The culmination of losing so much in such a short period time caused me to fall into a deep depression. I sought counseling only to be led to a life of popping pills. There was medicine to help me sleep, wake up, calm nerves, speed up nerves and the like. I later would use the medicine that was supposed to help bring me out of darkness, to try to take my own life.

My heart was broken and empty and I knew something was missing. My depressed state triggered my heart to realize it had a huge hole that could only be filled by accepting Jesus Christ as my Lord and Savior.

There have been many challenges during my walk. Those who have walked with me have asked "How is it that you aren't crazy?" There was the battle with depression. My money was funny. But the major challenge came on Sunday, April 16, 2006 at 8:00 pm. This was the day a doctor told me that my thirteen-year-old daughter was dead.

It was Resurrection Sunday and by all standards, it was a perfect day. I had sweet talked my daughter into wearing a dress and to put on a little lip gloss. My daughter was an athlete and had no interest in being a frou-frou girly girl. She was absolutely beautiful and had a hard time with all of the attention that she was receiving at church from everyone. We had made our way to the family gathering to have dinner. The home was full of love and laughter.

My daughter was outside with the other kids playing. One of the children ran into the house and said my daughter had wet herself. I walked outside and my baby was lying face down on the ground not responding to my call. My heart sank.

I turned her over and saw what no parent wanted to see. My baby was gone and clinically I knew this, but as a mother, I would not accept it. I yelled for someone to help me and to call 911. I began CPR on my baby and thought "She is gone, she is gone! GOD! PLEASE don't take my baby away from me."

The ambulance finally arrived after what seemed like an eternity. As I sat in the ambulance, I heard God ask me, "Do you believe?" "YES, I believe." I said emphatically. I thought that God was going to raise my daughter on that day. He had another plan, because the following Saturday, we buried my daughter.

What is amazing about this entire situation is what God had instructed me to do prior to the loss of my daughter. He had instructed the entire household to go on a forty-day Daniel fast. The day the fast had ended was Resurrection Sunday.

I wish I could say that continuing to live after the loss of my daughter was the only major challenge I have had to face. There have been plenty.

Just 2011 alone brought an explosion in my neighbor's apartment that caused me and eight of my neighbors to lose our homes. After the fire, I had to rely on my friends to provide a roof over my head. In the midst of being temporarily homeless, my two-year relationship ended and the stress of being hit with so many things at once resulted in a miscarriage.

The challenge of being obedient to God and trusting Him in all of the chaos was difficult. I would pray and ask God for direction but I could not hear Him through the constantly asked question "What are you going to do?" I was surprised at how angry those six words made me. I had no idea of what I was going to do.

My greatest accomplishment during this time was to get out of bed and celebrate the victory of having my feet touch the floor.

There were so many people offering their advice, yet the more I listened to them, the more confused I became. I knew they all meant well, but what I needed was to hear God. I longed for Him to tell me why He had me to go through this Job experience. Yet, through it all, my heart knew that God was with me every step of the way.

Today, I am still learning and growing. Have I made mistakes and bad choices? Of course I have. However, my mistakes and choices have helped to shape me into the woman I am today.

Every day is another opportunity to experience something new. I endured some pretty tough things, but God has kept me in the midst of them all.

Every experience has created a drive in me to keep walking and to seek God even more. I have learned the value of saying "no" and make no excuses for it. God has opened my eyes to see myself the way that He sees me. With His guidance, I have moved from grace to grace and glory to glory, through the valleys, in the wilderness, and on top of the mountains. Each experience has built faith in God's Word, hope for tomorrow, and an expectation for His best.

My deepest desire from God is for Him to never stop amazing me. I don't want to get to the point where I become conditioned to what God does in my life. I don't want to take for granted hearing the birds sing or feeling the wind blow.

I also would one day love to get married and start a family when He sees fit. Parts of my life read as though it is a modern day version of the book of Job. I stand in expectation that my latter rain will be greater than my former rain (Scripture).

My testimony came from a conversation I had with my Pastor's wife at our annual women's retreat. She asked me how I was able to walk in six inch stiletto heels. My response was, *"I have learned how to walk through the hurt."*

I don't know about you, but I love a cute pair of shoes. Sometimes, you find a pair that fits perfectly, yet after a few hours they begin to become a little uncomfortable. You realize that if you sit for a little while, the pain eases and you are able to begin your walk again.

Sister, your walk with God is sometimes like this. Proverbs 3: 5-6 says *"Trust in the Lord with all your heart and lean not on your own understanding; in all your ways acknowledge him, and he will make your paths straight."*

There will be pain, there will be times when it seems like everything is flowing perfectly, and there will be times when you want to stop and just take off your "shoes." During the times when life seems to come at you with every obstacle, this is when you can rest assured that God is with you.

To know God intimately requires discipline, dedication, sacrifice and obedience. Intimacy takes time to develop and in order to develop something, you must invest time and as Psalm 46:10 says *"Be still, and know that I am God."*

With all the distractions of the world it is easy to be consumed by our environment and miss what God is trying to teach. Make time daily to study God's Word. Find a place where you can kick off your shoes and just be consumed by His presence.

Surround yourself with people who will provoke you to righteousness and sharpen you. Proverbs 27:17 reminds us *"As iron sharpens iron, so one man sharpens another."* These people should be those who are either at a point in their walk with Christ that you desire to be or someone who is walking the journey with you.

These people should be able to speak life and truth to you in love. They should not be afraid to correct you when you are wrong, encourage you when you are down, and help to redeem you when you fall. There is definitely strength in numbers and the more support you have in your walk; the more you will see how far you have come. These people serve as a supplement to God, not His replacement.

Remember, this journey is not a competition and everyone's journey is different. God created you specifically for His purpose and you do have purpose! No one can complete your assignment.

Jesus Died for That, Too!
Sexual Impurity

Patrica Allbritton

I always had a deep desire to strengthen my relationship with God. It was about the spring of 1984, I was approaching my twentieth birthday.

I was in the military for about two years. My fellow sailor and friend invited me to go to church with her one Sunday morning. I can remember that day like it was yesterday. I was waiting for her to pick me up and take me to her church.

I always enjoyed going to church but this time it was going to be different. I had the spirit of expectancy all over me and before the service was over, I had accepted Christ and learned about eternal life.

I had come from another faith. This experience was different; it was about relationship instead of legalism. The pastor asked this question on the day I accepted Christ into my life, *"if I was to die right now did I know where I would spend eternity?"*

I tried to come up with an answer in my mind. The pastor began to teach from the Bible where I would spend eternity. In the middle of service, I was puzzled because I thought I already the answer because of my church teachings as a child.

As a child I went to church with my mother. I had served her God. I sang in the choir and went to Bible study with my mother.

I discovered when worldly influences came my way that I did not have a personal relationship with Christ. What I knew was religion, but this did not help me to strengthen my walk with Christ.

Time and time again I found myself imprisoned by my choices. One of my mentors talked about how the media influences our emotions. This would influence my decisions concerning boys, then later men.

I realized that I would not find "Mr. Right" until I found a personal relationship with Jesus Christ. Why? My expectations were so high and they could not be met. I did not understand the truth until I suffered much discord in my relationships. I was wounded, disillusioned and angry and I went on a quest to seek therapy from this major challenge in my life.

I found out through my personal relationship with Jesus that you cannot be a prisoner, without your permission; knowledge is power. While that statement is true you must be able to handle or process

that power. You can quote purity related material or attend singles'
or marriage enrichment conferences but you must take action to
avoid commit sexual immorality.

You must make a covenant with your eyes not to take in
pornography or lust in any form. This takes a conscious effort
because mostly everything that is advertised uses some form of lust
or pornography to sell their products.

You must make a covenant with your ears to abstain from music
that will entice you to want to participate in lustful acts. You must
make a covenant with your mouth that you will abstain from corrupt
communication that will lead you to engage in lustful or profane
communication. You must make a covenant with your hands, your
lips, and your sex organs not to have sex before marriage. I know
this is easier said than done.

The Bible declares *"that if any person lacks wisdom, ask God
and He will give it to you"* James 1:5. The Holy Spirit will help you
to stay pure if you will tap into the His power. However, to be free
from sexual impurities, you must want to be free.

I had challenges in relationships. I was truly codependent. I
was driven to total despair through my bad relationship choices
because of my destructive sexual thoughts and behaviors. Lust was

the driving force behind my acting out. I was seeking someone to love me and to fill the void of emptiness in my life because I did not know what love truly meant.

Through therapy I found out that the spiritual sickness of lust wanted sexual stimulation instead of God's love. I had learned after many years of abusing my body, my mind, and my spirit that lust wanted anything other than what was best for me.

I wondered how I could live without lust. It became clear that all I had to do was give it up. I doubted that life without lust was possible. I found out that there was hope in God. I learned that progressive victory over lust was possible. I had learned to call on God for help. I leaned on the support of those who shared common issues with lustful desires; yet, desired healthy and pure relationships.

Yes in 1984, I had surrendered my life to Christ but in that area particularly I thought I could handle without God's help. I learned that I was leaning on my own understanding. Thanks to God for His grace and His mercy. He knew what was best for me. Over twenty years I had let God down, in and out of unhealthy relationships. I knew that God had someone prepared special for me.

God wants us healed from broken relationships just as much as He wants us healed from a dreadful disease. Sexual impurity is a dreadful disease and it does not care who it attacks. God is no respecter of persons. What He has done for others He can do and will do for you.

Today, I have come full circle; I am with the love of my life, my best friend, my fiancé. It is my desire the share the challenges and obstacles that I have been through, to help bring other women to wholeness.

God's grace will restore us to right thinking in the area of dating and long term relationships even if we had failed before. By the grace of God, as an Evangelist, entrepreneur and a veteran of the military, I am sharing with my sisters His plan for wholeness for his children, if healing and wholeness is what we desire.

My deepest desire from God is for me to have my own ministry. My desire is to heal the broken hearted and those suffering from lust in all forms so that they can live free from bondage. If you desire a healthy relationship, I wish to help you to be free from lust so that you can enjoy the journey here on earth while preparing for a life of eternity.

God restores so there is no sin so shameful that He can't restore you to wholeness and give you the desires of your heart. As the Samaritan Woman, you can proudly proclaim, *"Come see a man that healed me from my* sexual impurity!" Yes, Jesus touched her spirit and delivered her and she ran to share that God healed *her from sexual impurity.*

In John 4:4-27, when Jesus' disciples left and went into the city of Samaria to buy food; Jesus was tired from ministering and from His journey in Judea and from Galilee so He sat by the well until they returned from the city. A woman from Samaria approached the well to draw water and noticed Jesus resting.

Jesus spoke to the woman at the well and asked her for a drink. The woman was alarmed and knew that there was something special about Jesus because He did not seek to violate her as the other men had done. Jesus spoke wisdom into her life. He did not use the woman.

The Samaritan woman did not know He was the son of God. Jesus witnessed and told her about Himself and also He let her know that he was aware of her past. Jesus talked to her like He came alive to me and shared the relationship and beauty of true worship with her as He did with me.

Jesus died to save us from our sins. He *died for sexual impurity* and I thank God because now I am free!

What Becomes of the Broken Hearted?

Nicolle Brazil

S ome memories of my childhood are so vivid. Images come to mind, along with experiences, some good and some bad. I remember playing in my first basketball game, my first school play, and the first time my dad took me to McDonalds. My first Holy Communion is one of those memorable events.

I will never forget standing before God, the priest, my parents, teachers, and friends and family and accepting Christ through communion. Imagine my surprise when they passed the same cup of wine for each student to take a drink. One cup!

I remember having to go to confession and tell the priest all my sins. Being Catholic was hard. It required complete submission to a very strict environment. But it was what I was told to do.

Everything I learned about God was mostly at school and to be honest, I didn't feel like I had a choice. If you go to Catholic school, you follow their rules. Although I went to Catholic school, and was obedient as a child to this faith, I also attend a Presbyterian Church a few doors down from my house.

I would attend a Baptist Church with my auntie. Religion was all around me, mostly by direction of someone else. It was in me though, church, and God. I felt it! But honestly, I was confused. Whose way is right? Where do I fit in? So that's what I became, a "fitter inner."

I did everything I was told to do to be a good little Catholic girl. It wasn't until many years later, after a tragic life-changing situation occurred that I choose to really give my life to Christ. Before then, I thought life was good, normal, and I was doing great. And it was. But the moment I made that personal choice, all hell broke loose.

When I was twenty-four years old, I fell in love. Oh my, how I fell. Not only did I fall for him, but I fell deep into sin.

I had never had a real boyfriend because Sister Mary Catherine made sure we knew about hell and how you got there. And a boy before marriage was one sure way! I never forgot that.

I decided I wanted to forget what she said. Not only did I want to forget, I chose to totally ignore all the things I had learned about God and His word. Now, I still went to church, but I was not living according to God's word. I was chasing this boy all over town. I was following him, sinning with him, drinking, having sex, skipping work and just lost my mind.

I knew it was wrong, but it felt good. And God would still love me and forgive me and then later, I would get myself together.

The more I did it the more I felt my soul dying. But hey, this guy loved me and I felt important! I was no longer the nerd with glasses, the overweight girl with the long hair; the girl with the strict father.

I was trying to live life without following the rules I knew so well. I was trying to fit in somewhere and this place felt real nice. Every young person my age was living like this. I had always struggled to fit in so this was what I wanted - to belong.

I knew I was headed for trouble. I knew I was going against God's plans. But, IT FELT GOOD! And even though I couldn't stand the person I had become inside, outside I was looking like I was happy. It was all good because this beautiful young man loves me.

I still invited my boyfriend to attend church with me. We would talk about God. I would try to share that part of my life with Him. But he was lost, and I was losing myself. I did not know that God would soon take this man from my life.

That man I loved was shot and killed right before my very eyes. When he died that day, a piece of me died. This was not happening! Never did I imagine the change that would happen after that day.

It came slowly and in the meantime, I was devastated! I questioned God over and over. Why LORD! I was depressed, I considered suicide, and I just felt like I was dead. I hurt so badly. The pain was unbearable. My heart was broken, I was broken.

I had faced other issues in my life. I had felt unwanted, unloved, and unnecessary. I had witnessed my parents' terrible separation, but they got back together. I had been teased as a young girl for being overweight, but I lost weight. I had many things happen to cause me pain, but nothing hurt me to the core like witnessing the death of my first love. Nothing left me as empty as this, so cheated.

What do I do now? Who is going to love me? Who was I going to love? Who was I going to share all my time with? I asked many questions of God. While asking and trying to just get through the day without breaking down, God spoke to my spirit, "I will love you."

He asked me, *"Will you love me? Will you give me all the time and energy you gave this man? Will you follow me like you followed him? Will you remember who I am? I am your first love. I am your Lord."*

Right there, on that floor in my bedroom, in my momma's house, I GAVE MY LIFE TO CHRIST! I cried and prayed, "Lord, if you just help me make it through this night alive, I will give my life to you." God saved me on that night. He saved my life. He touched me and held me and from that night on, I promised to give Him my all.

It took me years to get through that time of grieving. Years of pain, searching, questioning God, asking for forgiveness for giving that man all I owed to the Lord.

I was also dealing with insecurities, fears, and doubts I had about life. I had to deal with where I fit in this life, abandonment issues, everything that had happened to me. Challenges I had all my life forced their way in to make company for my already broken heart.

I felt unloved. Wanting to be loved was the most important need in my life. As I look back on so many of my trials, I realize how very broken I was even before my boyfriend's death.

His death was a way for God to speak to me in my brokenness and He told me to LIVE! He showed me how much He loved me and that no one else could give me what He could give me.

I began to examine my life, my goals, my dreams and I chose to live. I went back to church regularly. God sent me my husband. I had my first son. I went back to school and obtained my BA in Psychology and my MA in Community Counseling.

I began to live the life God had intended for me. I knew it all the time but I had to experience that so that God could reach me in my pain. I was severely broken. If it hadn't been for that traumatic experience, I may have never turned to the Lord the way I did.

Today, I am a changed woman. Nothing is perfect and while I have different challenges; I have a strong faith in God. I have learned to listen to God and abide in His word. I know He is a healer of hearts. I know He loves me. I know that He wants the best for me and my family, which now includes three beautiful sons.

I know how to seek Him in the darkest times. I am more confident because I know how God turned my life around. I opened my broken heart to the Lord, and He now permanently abides there. I know HIS love is the most important love I can receive. I know I serve a perfect God who is available and able to help me through the darkest hours.

My deepest desire was to be loved, embraced, and accepted. God has given me that and much more. He has shown me that HE is the lover of my soul, my friend, my LORD, my savior. He can make my life worth living. God helped me to see myself the way He sees me. This love that God gives is irreplaceable. There is none like Him! No person on this earth can love me like the Lord. There is no place I fit better than in His will.

"The sacrifices of a God are a broken spirit, a broken and a contrite heart, these, O God, You will not despise" (Psalm 51:17). I hope to share this with women, young and old, who are looking for worth in relationships. If you are looking to fit in or struggling to love yourself, in a place of brokenness, a place of pain, hurt depression and self-defeat, or if you feel unworthy, if you feel broken, God wants to meet you there.

There you will find much more than you can ever imagine. The most important relationship you can have is with God. There you will find an amazing LOVE! A love so sincere and gentle, a love so pure and patient, a love so wise and HOLY! *"The LORD is near to those who have a broken heart, and saves such as have a contrite spirit"* (Psalm 34:18).

The LOVE of God mends all broken hearts! Won't you give Jesus the key to your heart today?

Desire God's Smile

Apostle Candace Ford

I am a thirty-five year old woman who came to Christ at the ripe old age of nineteen. Some memories of my childhood are so vivid. Images come to mind, along with experiences, some good and some bad. Although I was born to parents who were Christians, I didn't have an understanding of my salvation as a child.

I knew that we attended church, that we fellowshipped with other church members, we sang, we had Sunday school, but I did not understand the importance of salvation, the sacrifice of Jesus or the joy of having a true, real relationship with the God-head.

I did not realize that I was bound until we were forced out of the church when I was nineteen. The pastor gave my mother a choice to commit an illegal act or be removed from the ministry. She chose to walk in integrity, so we moved our membership to another church.

After joining this church, I began to experience a level of spiritual freedom, cultivation and growth that I had not experienced before. There was liberty to worship, freedom to pray all within the divine order that a church should operate.

Our pastor functioned fully as a teacher and had a heart of a shepherd, desiring his flock to have an intimate relationship with God, not just on Sundays but on an everyday basis.

After visiting for a few Sundays, I saw teenagers my age involved in worship, prayer and calling out to God. I desired the very thing in which they had, I desired the Holy Spirit. I desired Him. I asked the Lord to receive and I did.

After the baptism of the Holy Spirit, I knew my life had been changed. I knew that my prayers were different, my understanding of the Word of God became clearer and I began to understand that I had a call on my life to intercede for others, to teach and to lead others into their purpose with God.

As I fellowshipped more in the ministry and begin to seek God, study more, pray more, I understood that as a child, my family and I were spiritually manipulated by our former pastor.

Our salvation and walk with Christ was not important. What was important was that we did whatever she said do, even if that meant going against the word of God. We were slaves to what she wanted, even though Jesus had given us life and freedom through His sacrifice.

I do believe that is why so many run from church because man has used the Bible to manipulate control and keep you in bondage. Galatians 5:1 reads, *"It is for freedom that Christ has set us free, Stand firm, then, and do not let yourselves be burdened again by a yoke of slavery."*

When Christ set us free and we accepted Him as our Lord and Savior, no man can put us back in that bondage. It is up to us to stand firm, study the word, cultivate our relationship with Christ so that we will not allow anyone, not even ourselves, to put us in spiritual jail.

Knowing what the Word says and willing to apply it to your life will keep you from making the mistakes my parents did in staying a member of that church. But it was a learning process, for how can you truly appreciate freedom, unless you have been bound?

I believe my major challenge during my walk was becoming secure in who God had called me to be. God does not give you your story 100%, so as you walk with Him there are many times of being unsure and insecure, especially when you may not have the total support of those around you.

I struggled in my walk with not being validated by spiritual leaders in my calling. I struggled with accepting who I was in the

Kingdom of God. I struggled with recognizing my gifts and abilities because of lack of knowledge and understanding of how the gifts should operate.

When you don't know who you are, you will allow others to label you, manipulate you or choose the path in which they feel you should walk. This was my case, because I wasn't secure, I would try to fit in, try to please, try to take care of everyone else's business and put my own on the back burner.

Because I didn't know my true identity in Christ, I constantly threw my pearls to the swine. I would work on ministry projects, do all the work, pay the bill and never be acknowledge. Not that I look for the recognition of man, but if I had known who I was and my importance I would have discerned more, what to be a part of and what not to be a part.

I believe when you know who you are there is a certain standard that you live by, a benchmark that allows you to align yourself with like minded people, places and things. This security prevents you from being used and manipulated into something you don't want to do.

My biggest fete was feeling condemned by the church when I entered into a relationship and conceived a child out of wedlock.

Although I had committed the sin of fornication, sex outside of marriage (Gal 5:19) and I had asked God for forgiveness, man was very judgmental.

Many of the *"church folks,"* people I believe know of God only through religion and not relationship, celebrated in my mistake and turn their backs on me during a very confusing season of my life.

At that time I felt alone, I was depressed, had thoughts of suicide and it set me back years of spiritual security. Although I understood it was my choice to sin and to make the mistake, I never thought that my mistake would be the very thing that would propel me into a greater love for God. In this time God began to show me how important His love was and moreover how important it was to show God's love to others.

My walk with God today is 100% different then what it was. I feel I am more security in who I am because I have been given identity through my spiritual covering. I am an Apostle of the Lord and it is my responsibility to encourage, edify, break up, build up and pull down.

I understand that I am to assist others in discovering their purpose in God and give them the tools in which to reach their destiny. In this season of my life I can honestly say I trust God with all my heart on a day by day basis. I believe God at His word and I trust that He will provide for me in everything that I endeavor to do.

There are some days that I am in awe of the accelerated growth through the Holy Spirit. I am comfortable in my own skin, no longer concerned about what man thinks of me, but simply wanting to please God with my life and my worship. Knowing that I am on this earth to assist other women in knowing who they are, knowing I am a leader for leaders, in business as well as in ministry. It keeps me focused on my personal and business alignments. It keeps me humble because without Christ, His love, His sacrifice and His wisdom, I could not be me!

I desire to please God in everything that I do. I want Him to be pleased with my work, my ministry for Him, my raising my children, and my submission to my husband.

I want God to be able to smile on my doings while I'm earth and not only when I get to the judgment seat. I desire to love God with all my heart and soul and to do what He has called me to do.

My deepest desire is to obey God, to trust God and to always be willing to go the next level in Him. I believe that this next level is a greater season of worship, a more financially stable place for my family and simply to live by faith and dwell in God's peace.

Many times as women we are so concerned about others and their needs but in this next level of God, I know He is going to teach and train me how to take care of myself so that I can be more of an asset to others. He is going to teach me how to feed myself spiritually so that I may give that same truth to others. He will teach me how to walk in faith through situations so that I can assist others to the same.

I love God because I know that if it were not for Him I would not have peace in chaotic situations. I would not have joy when bad days seem horrible and I would not have grace to keep me from falling into condemnation.

Walking with God is not an easy task. It takes patience, love, long-suffering and faith, things we need to mature us. If you desire to know God more intimately you must come to the end of yourself. You must put God first and everything else last. You must allow Him to give you wisdom and understanding. You must allow the Holy Spirit to reveal His word for your life.

Finally, you cannot be afraid of God, yes we must have a reverential fear (respect) of the Lord and His awesomeness. We cannot be afraid to be transparent with Him.

We must tell Him all of our fears, concerns, what we worry

about and questions that we have concerning our purpose. God is our Father and He loves us so there is no need to hold back from Him.

God tells us to seek His face evermore, to seek His strength (1 Chronicles 16:11). Be steadfast in your intimate relationship with Him so that He can show you the truest form of who He is...*desire His smile.*

A New Song to Sing

Sara Robillard

I wake up one morning with no desire to rise. As I stare at the clock, minutes ticking away, dark thoughts begin to eat away at the edges of my mind. What is the point? What reason is there for me to keep on living? Nothing is ever going to change.

God has abandoned me and I am trapped in despair. We had been raised to be "Christians." We attended church, listened to television and radio sermons, and had family bible studies, but there lacked any connection with the heart. We had head knowledge, but it was all for show. It served as a mask, hiding the deep, dark secret that encompassed our lives at home.

For years, I prayed to God, begging Him for some kind of deliverance. What amazes me is that despite the abuse and dysfunction within our home and how God's word was so often twisted and distorted to justify crime it was in the end that His truth broke through the lies spoke to my heart, leading me back to Christ.

My stepfather was physically abusive to my siblings and me when we were younger. He was violent, demeaning and controlling, playing vicious mind games with our tender minds. I never knew what to expect coming home from school or when he'd get home from work late at night. He worked as a security officer at a local college, and later went on to graduate from the police academy.

I remember my sister and I lying awake in tears and listening as he would take out his rage on my brother in the next room while our mother looked on. We labored under the unspoken truth that no matter what, we were "damned if we did, damned if we didn't." He crushed our self esteem, and instilled fear within us.

Early one autumn morning, during my middle school years, I was literally pulled out of bed to rake the leaves in the front of the yard. I began work without any breakfast, and soon began to feel sick.

Despite my fears, I went and knocked on my parent's bedroom door to tell them I wasn't feeling well. I was pulled in and had a thermometer stuck in my mouth. In a rage, my stepfather picked me up and threw me against the closet door. When the thermometer broke in my mouth, he suddenly became concerned and stopped to make sure I hadn't swallowed any of the mercury. Once it was assured I hadn't, I was given a bowl of corn flakes and sent back to work.

As we aged, his physical abuse became more aimed towards my younger brother, and he began his sexual abuse towards my sister and me. He cut us off from our relations, and pulled me out of school to keep me at home.

My stepfather molested me for over ten years, and was somehow able to justify "our relationship," as he called it. I carried conviction, but if I dared to bring it to his attention, he always turned the tables on me.

Confusion overwhelmed me. Was *I* the real "user" in all of this? Was my abuser truly sincere? Did he really love me the way he said he did? Was I being punished for not feeling the same?

God seemed to be on his side, not mine. The conflict destroyed me on the inside and as I learned more of the depths of my abuser's depravity, I fell deeper into despair; if I wasn't praying earnestly for his death, I literally cursed at God.

While the words of Christ about forgiveness (Luke 6:37) echoed in the back of my mind, I mastered justifying my bitter attitude. My abuser didn't deserve forgiveness, he deserved my hatred, and I was enslaved by it.

I was an incessant liar – critical and hypocritical. I was addicted to violence and sensuality. I was filled with hatred and bitterness, and abused those nearest to me. Even more so, I was deeply depressed, lonely and filled with hopelessness.

Everything had reached a climax, and I knew I was at a fork in the road. After years of misery, I was ready for it to end. I believed all hope was gone, but for some reason, something deep within wouldn't let go. God had already begun to chip away at the walls around my heart.

I had lately begun to listen to the music of a particular Christian artist, and found myself clinging to the truth God was expressing through it. I had cried myself to sleep on several nights listening to a certain song as it assured me that there was always hope. I couldn't allow myself to believe that, even though I was desperate for it. The only reason I got out of bed that morning was to listen to one of this artist's songs. Beyond that, I wasn't sure what I was going to do, but God knew. As I listened, the Spirit brought to mind a scripture so well known:

"For I know the plans that I have for you,' declares the LORD, 'plans for welfare and not for calamity to give you a future and a hope. Then you will call upon Me and come and pray to Me, and I will listen to you. You will seek Me and find Me when you search for Me with all your heart. I will be found by you,' declares

the LORD" (Jeremiah 29:11-14).

To this day, it's hard to describe what took place in my heart in those profound moments, but the resentment and hatred was replaced by a hope in God's promises. I had finally realized I was *letting* myself be controlled by my hate, and because I was letting myself be controlled, I was *losing* out on all God had promised me. It made the crimes committed against me no less wrong, but I had to take responsibility for how I was responding and choose to forgive.

I found such freedom in obedience. The wedge between me and my Father in Heaven lifted. I found myself hungry for change...and little did I realize how quickly the change would come.

Through divine circumstances, God delivered me. The recovery process has been difficult at times, but God continues to mend me, stripping away the unhealthy mentalities left behind by my past.

A Godly friend and mentor put it this way: *"Picture yourself in a room with walls painted blue. All your life, you've been told that the walls were yellow, and now you are beginning to see them for what they really are: blue."* When you've been so conditioned to believe one thing, and suddenly your eyes are opened, it can be wonderful and exciting; but in the next breath, it can bring about such fear and uncertainty."

I had been told many lies all my life, and even once freed; I tended to focus more on the counterfeit than the truth. Lies can be overwhelming, which is why truth – God's word – has become so valuable to me. Through it, God reveals Who He Is.

I've come to realize that He is all that I need, and my greatest desire is to know Him more. His love for me is complete and perfect. My love for Him reaches greater depths as I study His word, learning how I can express my love for Him through obedience (1 John 2:3-6).

I had long struggled with either dwelling on the past, or being too focused on the future; as a result, I was blinded to what God had placed before me. God had to correct that in me because it's in each precious moment that we find opportunities to give Him glory.

I've found myself clinging closer and closer to God, my Father, my Abba. I have learned the meaning behind the declaration of Job: *"The LORD gave and the LORD has taken away. Blessed be the name of the LORD." (1:21b, NASB)* To borrow words from Oswald Chambers, *"He can crumple me up or exalt me; He can do anything He chooses."*

Before the world began, before God set everything into motion, He knew what would take place in Eden. Before He spoke a word, before anything was given life, Jesus saw the cross. And yet, despite all that, He created the world anyway. Why? To quote another familiar verse: *"For God so loved the world, that He gave His only begotten Son, that whoever believes in Him shall not perish, but have eternal life." (John 3:16, NASB)*

Through His word and His people I have begun to know true love – the love of God. Today, I find great confidence and hope in the promises found in Psalm 40:1-3: *"I waited patiently for the LORD and He inclined to me and heard my cry. He brought me up out of the pit of destruction, out of the miry clay, and He set my feet upon a rock making my footsteps firm. He put a new song in my mouth, a song of praise to our God; many will see and fear and will trust in the LORD." (NASB)*

I was overwhelmed by my own reflection in these verses. I heard my cries to God through all the years of abuse, and even though I had felt they went no farther than the ceiling, God was listening. In His own way and in His own time did He deliver me, and I continue to experience greater freedom and healing.

He has literally put a *"new song"* on my lips. As I write my own lyrics in hopes that someday others may hear and know the hope that is in God. In the same way I received it by hearing through the song of another. There was a time when I despised my life and experiences, but I have come to see how the God of all things can take even my pain and turn it into something for His glory – something beautiful.

And this promise extends to every one of His chosen people.

My Journey to Wholeness
Shakia Mosley

I gave my life completely to Christ November 2010. The Holy Ghost fell on me in my life has never been the same. I was drowning in heartache and pain. I finally came to the end of myself and realized I am nothing without Jesus.

I have three kids from three different men. None of them turned out to be what I always hoped for; when I was a little girl. My last son's dad was the last straw for me. After being manipulated, humiliated, verbally abused, and scorned, I was through.

I tried to ease the hurt by turning to drugs (crack cocaine), alcohol abuse, but by then the damage was done. I was on the path to destruction. I ended up going to jail. Child protective services was in and out of my life. I could not take it anymore. I had given up on life. One day a friend of mine, who was actually my powder (cocaine) buddy, led me to church. I could not take it anymore. I realized I needed help, serious help or I was going to die.

I experienced low self-esteem and learning how to forgive myself as well as others. When I was growing up I felt like the black sheep of the family.

My parents conceived me while they were in an adulterous relationship. It was hard to have a father who was married to another woman. As years went on; I grew older and became aware how unwanted I was by the way my mother treated me. My sisters from my dad's first marriage despised me. I had a void of love in my life; a black hole.

When I turned sixteen, I ran away from home and became pregnant with my first child. My pregnancy was totally unexpected emotionally and mentally. I felt like for once I would have someone to love me back (my baby).

I must say the different relationships and family issues were tugging at my very soul. All I knew was I needed help and I needed help fast. I thank God that he kept His hands on me.

I have learned a lot about life and love. The road is not easy, but I know God has a great plan. He knows my beginning and my end.

I suffered at the hands of abuse; physically and mentally. The abuse was so dramatic. I suffered a major injury to my head. I had to go to the hospital and receive stitches. The paramedic that responded to the scene stated, "I was lucky to be alive."

When I finally found the courage to leave; I could not do it nicely. The guy was a thin line between crazy and insane. During this time I and my dad were meeting up every day. My dad was helping me get my child to school and back. I knew he carried a three fifty-seven (weapon) with him in his truck, under the seat. I snuck the weapon in my purse and I said to myself, "I am determined to get away from the maniac that considered me his girl. I don't know what kind of love this was, but it was not what I wanted.

I knew then it was either him or me; my mind was made up. The next time he threatened me I gathered all my strength and held the weapon up and told him, "Don't take another step towards me." The fool actually thought I was bluffing. I felt my hand squeeze the trigger and missed. After that incident he knew I had taken back control of my life.

Today I am strong, courageous and full of life. I am a woman who has found the love of her life (Jesus), after all the years of heartache and pain. I realize the Lord was there all along; waiting for my safe return home. In his arms is where I belong.

I am so very thankful for the good Lord. His amazing grace is the song in my heart. Whenever I sit and flashback over all the trials and tribulation, I can see how it was Jesus who held on to me.

I believe you have to go through some things, so you can know that Jesus is the way, the truth, and the light. I have a greater appreciation for life and Jesus Christ. I am happily enjoying the benefits of being a daughter of the King.

I am reminded of the story of "Beauty and the Beast." My heart was longing for my prince all my life. I could never see what was in front of me all those years. I have truly found my heart's desire.

My deepest desire was to find love. I found it in Jesus. When I needed courage and strength, Jesus died and rose. He showed me He was my courage and strength. When I thought I could not make it another day. Jesus whispered in my ear, *"You will survive."*

As women living in a society where makeup, expensive clothes, coca cola shape bodies are popular. We can get discouraged and feel like we are not worthy enough to be loved.

My sisters, "That is a BIG lie from the enemy!" God created us with the word of His mouth. God spoke the world into existence and said, "It is good." It is good, means you are too!

You may have messed up in your past, but your past is your stepping stone to your future. Respect God's word and know that His word is true. You will begin to respect yourself also. God did not design us to be restricted in our minds because of lack of love, misfortune, abuse, etc.

Get up today and speak over yourself. The rain has gone away and you have a new day. Let the light of God's word shine through you; let it penetrate those hard places in your life. The places where you don't want anyone to know about.

You can go to the throne of grace and lay all your burdens at the masters' feet. *The Lord tells us he will throw our sins into the sea of forgetfulness.* No matter where you are or what you have done; begin your journey to Holiness, with the only one Who can make you whole! You will be happy you did.

Without God, Where Would I Be

Stacey Shaw Virgo

From an early age, I always knew what the inside of church looked like, what it means to not to miss church on a Sunday. Living with my aunt, I rarely missed Sunday school or church until I decided to move out on my own at the age of twenty after given birth to my son. The worldly secular life style took me over for thirteen years which I thought was some of the best years of my life with a few down moments.

It was not until March 2006 while I was driving in my car one Wednesday afternoon when I received a call from my son. He told me that he was going to be suspended from school and I needed to get to the school office right away. This is when things began to change significantly in my life. On this particular day, I went to the school only to find out that my son was being accused of taking something from another child. He told me he didn't, and as his mother I believed him.

There was a sheriff on the school compound who told me that if he does not admit to taking the item, he would be sent to boot camp.

I saw where I would be losing my son and at that very moment I did not know what to do.

The school gave me until the following day to speak to him to find out exactly what had taken place. I returned the following morning to the school with my son who was still indicating that he did not take the item.

While I was sitting down in the school office, I felt something come over me and I realized he was not telling me the truth. I looked at him and I held him in my arms and said, I don't want to lose you, please, please tell the truth. "Do you want them to take you away from me? He said no. I looked at him I said son, I love you, no one will hurt you, I am here for you, please tell them the truth.

I was so scared, I saw my baby being sent away and there was nothing I could do. I sat down in that chair and I remembered that it would take a miracle to get him out of this situation. I turned to my son and began really pleading with him to tell the truth, within a few seconds I saw his emotions change and he finally admitted to me that the school was telling me the truth.

The sheriff turned to me and said, "I am so glad that he took responsibility, he will only have to serve in school suspension." I left the school and went in my car and knew that it was God who saved my baby. God is awesome, He is faithful.

The Sunday morning following the incident I woke up and I told my husband that the children and I will be going to church. This was the first in several years where I really had the desire to begin going back to church. I never knew that this was going to be the day that I would become a child of God, not just His creation but His child, His daughter, and His princess.

Listening to the sermon, the pastor was speaking about the rich man and the beggar, Lazarus (Luke 16:20-31) and he asked the congregation *"where would we be if we did not serve God."*

During the sermon he painted a scenario for us to think about which caused chills to run down my back. It was like he was speaking directly to me. I jumped up out of my seat and surrendered my life to the Lord. I had to make the decision to serve God.

Jesus does not force us to do anything. Everything we do is based on choices. One of these choices is either to choose life or death.

I went through six weeks of discipleship training and then I was baptized in December 2006. I was born again. The old person had passed away and all things were new.

Although it has been very rough, I have never looked back in terms of backsliding. Even when it crosses my mind, the sermon keeps coming back to me.

Don't think because you have surrendered your life to God that things will be much easier. The enemy does not like when souls are won for the Kingdom of God. The enemy will come with everything he has to distract you and to cause you to lose faith in God.

Read your bible, study the verses get a support group. You need to surround yourself with like minded people, who will guide and help you with your walk. When the rough days come, you will need to have that support. God will always be there for you, but He will also put His other children around you to help keep you on track.

Everything was going well until August 2006, when it all came crashing down. That morning my husband left due to circumstances beyond our control. I saw my children crying with so much pain. My son almost got into trouble again. I lost my house and had to give up a good job to try and save my family which did not work.

I lost the relationship with my birth father, money was running out, friends were gone and everything was literally pulled from me.

I began to feel so alone, the friends who I thought I had, were nowhere to be found. The families I thought I had, were nowhere to be found. I was left to pick up the pieces with two children and move on. I rented an apartment and I got a job where I worked for one year before I was laid off. My car was vandalized twice.

There were issues that were taking place in the church where I attended. I left, and hoped to never speak about it again.

After being laid off again in February 2008, with two children, I became employed again for eight months. I had to face employers who cursed in your face, spoke to you like you were garbage and had to work almost seven days a week.

Shortly before I was terminated from the job, I became ill. Parts of my body were burning. I suffered headaches for three months. My children had to call the paramedics for me early one morning. I was rushed to the hospital where I was then diagnosed with vertigo. During these times I keep on repeating Isaiah 53: 5 *"By his stripes I am healed."*

I was home for six months until I received another job in February 2008 and then was terminated in April 2008 due to a law suit the company was going through.

I have been admitted to the hospital twice since then. My son went through a series of tests because they thought he had leukemia. Six months later, he was diagnosed with scoliosis and that he required back surgery.

I saw God work for me so quickly that day. I called everyone

I knew and asked them to pray. I turned to my son and said, *"The devil is a liar. You will never have back surgery in the name of Jesus."* Within five minutes the head surgeon came in and said my son would not need surgery. That was God and only God. If it were not for God, my spiritual mother and a select group of people that God placed in my life, I do not know where I would be today.

There were nights when I would just cry. I would isolate myself from people, and wonder what I did wrong. I know I did not do anything wrong.

Yes, our choices have consequences, but Jesus said, He would never leave us nor forsake us. He said, "greater is He that is in me than he that is in the world."

Jesus says I am made in His image and likeness; I am Royalty, I am a Princess. Jesus died on the cross so that I may be redeemed from spiritual death, poverty and sickness. If my Father did all of that for me and He is the God of yesterday, today and forever.

I know that I will be able to break down all the barriers. During this time was when I also realized that I had put my husband on a high pedestal. I came to the realization that I now tell people, "Then My husband was my God.... But Now Jesus is My God."

Despite all the bumps, battles and challenges, I am still standing.

I have seen God work in my life and my children's life. There are days that I may break down; but one thing I have come to learn is that faith without works is dead.

If you have faith of a mustard seed you can move mountains. I will be breaking down my barriers. I am walking with God. I know that I am a solution to a problem here on the earth. I will achieve my purpose.

I am so highly blessed to know that I am a child of the living God. Being a mother is my greatest job. I have two extra ordinary children who are very loving. I thank God for each of them every day.

My father and I are slowly building back our relationship. My spiritual mother is always there to give me encouraging words and support me through the rough times. My pastors pray for me and support me in whatever way they can. I have friends that call me just to check up on me. I know without a shadow of a doubt I will receive seven times what the enemy has taken from me and my family.

I have always had a heart filled with compassion for people and helping others. I will be able to fulfill my purpose to show unconditional agape love to others. How can I not say I am blessed?

My deepest desire from God is know Him so that when I speak,

He speaks, when I pray, He is praying. When I speak words of healing, people are healed. I can write a check at any given time for someone in need once I receive approval from God. I know that my children, my husband and I have long healthy lives.

We will all receive a wonderful encounter with God. We will serve God better than the day before. We can be a significant blessing to others. When it is all over, we will all hear, *"Well done, my good and faithful servant."*

MAKE SURE GOD IS FIRST IN YOUR LIFE. Do not put anything before God, if you do (It does not matter if it is your husband, child, a job, your business… anything) He will remove it all from you so that you can depend on Him alone.

Once He is first in your life, then your family, your church and then your business/job. God is awesome. He is faithful and as long as you seek His kingdom first, you can never fail (Matthew 6:33). Be blessed and remember you are a solution to a problem, go after your dreams with the Holy Spirit leading your life.

There is no other place to be than with Him.

You Will Never Walk Alone
Scriptures for Your Journey

Psalm 103:12 As far as the east is from the west, So far has He removed our transgressions from us.

Isaiah 53:6 All we like sheep have gone astray; We have turned, every one, to his own way; And the LORD has laid on Him the iniquity of us all.

Matthew 19:24-26 And again I say to you, it is easier for a camel to go through the eye of a needle than for a rich man to enter the kingdom of God." [25]When His disciples heard *it,* they were greatly astonished, saying, "Who then can be saved?" [26]But Jesus looked at *them* and said to them, "With men this is impossible, but with God all things are possible."

Matthew 24:13 But he who endures to the end shall be saved.

Mark 1:15 and saying, "The time is fulfilled, and the kingdom of God is at hand. Repent, and believe in the gospel."

Mark 16:16 He who believes and is baptized will be saved; but he who does not believe will be condemned.

Luke 7:50 Then He said to the woman, "Your faith has saved you. Go in peace."

Luke 8:12 Those by the wayside are the ones who hear; then the devil comes and takes away the word out of their hearts, lest they should believe and be saved.

John 1:12 But as many as received Him, to them He gave the right to become children of God, to those who believe in His name:

John 3:16-17 For God so loved the world that He gave His only begotten Son, that whoever believes in Him should not perish but have everlasting life. [17] For God did not send His Son into the world to condemn the world, but that the world through Him might be saved.

John 5:34 Yet I do not receive testimony from man, but I say these things that you may be saved

John 8:36 Therefore if the Son makes you free, you shall be free indeed.

John 10:9 I am the door. If anyone enters by Me, he will be saved, and will go in and out and find pasture.

John 17:3 And this is eternal life, that they may know You, the only true God, and Jesus Christ whom You have sent.

Acts 2:21 And it shall come to pass that whoever calls on the name of the LORD shall be saved.

Acts 2:47 Praising God and having favor with all the people. And the Lord added to the church daily those who were being saved.

Acts 4:12 Nor is there salvation in any other, for there is no other name under heaven given among men by which we must be saved."

Acts 15:11 But we believe that through the grace of the Lord Jesus Christ we shall be saved in the same manner as they."

Acts 16:30-31 he brought them out and said, "Sirs, what must I do to be saved?" So they said, "Believe on the Lord Jesus Christ, and you will be saved, you and your household."

Romans 3:23 For all have sinned and fall short of the glory of God,

Romans 5:8-10 But God demonstrates His own love toward us, in that while we were still sinners, Christ died for us. [9] Much more then, having now been justified by His blood, we shall be saved from wrath through Him. For if when we were enemies we were reconciled to God through the death of His Son, much more, having been reconciled, we shall be saved by His life.

Romans 6:4 Therefore we were buried with Him through baptism into death, that just as Christ was raised from the dead by the glory of the Father, even so we also should walk in newness of life.

Romans 6:23 For the wages of sin *is* death, but the gift of God *is* eternal life in Christ Jesus our Lord.

Romans 10:9-10 That if you confess with your mouth the Lord Jesus and believe in your heart that God has raised Him from the dead, you will be saved. For with the heart one believes unto righteousness, and with the mouth confession is made unto salvation.

Romans 10:13 For whoever calls on the name of the LORD shall be saved.

2 Corinthians 5:17 Therefore, if anyone *is* in Christ, *he is* a new creation; old things have passed away; behold, all things have become new.

Ephesians 2:8-9 For by grace you have been saved through faith, and that not of yourselves; *it is* the gift of God, [9] not of works, lest anyone should boast.

Titus 3:5 Not by works of righteousness which we have done, but according to His mercy He saved us, through the washing of regeneration and renewing of the Holy Spirit.

Hebrews 9:27 And as it is appointed for men to die once, but after this the judgment...

1 Peter 3:18 For Christ also suffered once for sins, the just for the unjust, that He might bring us[a] to God, being put to death in the flesh but made alive by the Spirit…

1 John 1:9 If we confess our sins, He is faithful and just to forgive us *our* sins and to cleanse us from all unrighteousness.

1 John 2:6 He who says he abides in Him ought himself also to walk just as He walked.

1 John 4:19 We love Him because He first loved us.

1 John 5:11-13 And this is the testimony: that God has given us eternal life, and this life is in His Son. [12] He who has the Son has life; he who does not have the Son of God does not have life. [13] These things I have written to you who believe in the name of the Son of God, that you may know that you have eternal life, and that you may *continue to* believe in the name of the Son of God.

Revelation 3:20 Behold, I stand at the door and knock. If anyone hears My voice and opens the door, I will come in to him and dine with him, and he with Me.

Visionary Bio

Jaime L. Rohadfox, founder of Women of Divine Aspiration, LLC (WoDA) is a Christian author, coach, and speaker. Affectionately known as "Coach Jaime", she is passionate about empowering, edifying and equipping women to overcome their negative thinking and limited beliefs to unlock their potential, unleash their purpose and transform their deepest desires into their Divine destiny.

Jaime is no stranger to suffering from negative thinking and limited beliefs and God has used this to birth her ministry to help other women.

In addition to her ministry, she is a sought after book writing coach, helping women to deliver transparency when writing emotional stories. She often says, that "If you don't reveal it, God can't heal it." She believes satan uses one's inability to talk about the past as a weapon to steal, kill and to destroy destiny.

Jaime is also the author of her first self-published book, Give it Up Turn it Loose: A Woman's Journey from Dominion to Deliverance. This is a remarkable story of her determination to overcome the demons from her past.

To order your copy, please visit: http://giveitupturnitloose.com.

Jaime truly believes that one's testimony becomes their ministry and mission in life!

To learn more about Jaime L. Rohadfox, please visit her website: http://jaimelrohadfox.com. To learn more about Women of Divine Aspiration, LLC, please visit: http://womenofdivineaspiration.org.

Contributing Author Bios

Patrica Allbritton is a Native New Yorker, currently retired from the U.S. Navy. She is the visionary of Cover-Up Ministry where total health management is her business…first natural then spiritual. She stresses that God wants us whole in every area of our life. Patrica is also a licensed Evangelist through Visionaries In Covenant, Inc. She is a mentor, coach, friend, and mother to two adult sons, and pre-teen son. She can be found actively serving at Pentecostal Temple Ministries.

Effie Alofoje-Carr is a rapidly budding author, speaker and entrepreneur inspiring twenty-something from urban areas to sort out their issues and live their dreams. Effie holds a B.A. from Michigan State University and works as an advocate for victims of domestic violence in the city. A proud native of Detroit MI, if you need to survive your "quarter life crisis" and use the urban lifestyle to your advantage, she'll teach you how. Effie is an active member of Tabernacle of David Worship Center in Lansing, MI where she works with the women's ministry and serves as the children's ministry director.

Nicolle Brazil is a native of Pittsburgh, Pennsylvania. She has written a self-published children's book titled, You Can't Move an Elephant in One Day. Nicolle's passion for writing stems from childhood and she hopes to make a future in writing and publishing family-friendly books. She also enjoys writing stories with inspirational and spiritual themes. She is working on an inspiring adventure book geared towards teenagers. Her husband and their three sons are her inspiration and motivation to continue writing.

Lucinda Cross is a Lifestyle and Business fire starter specializing in women's success. She is the CEO and Founder of Activate!, Author of Corporate Mom Drop Outs, Founder of Praying Moms. org and Activate Me 24/7 Membership. She is also co-owner of the Super Mom Entrepreneur Conference and Expo. Her journey into entrepreneurship began when she became a mom and she has been building businesses ever since as a mompreneur. She has defied all the odds both in life and in business and has mastered the ability to turn adversities into advantages. She travels the world sharing her message and inspiring women to Activate in all areas of life!

Zarien Daniels is a dynamic speaker, play writer, motivator, teacher, counselor and divine leader. She is determined to empower women to walk within their divine destiny and purpose will of God for their lives. Ms. Daniels specializes within the mental health counseling field working with individuals suffering from acute mental health disabilities and is currently working to pursue her PhD in Clinical Psychology. Ms. Daniels is a blessed single parent of one son.

Reverend Barbara J. Elerby is a lover of the Lord. She focuses on the gift of His Peace. In her roles as a Certified Biblical Life Coach, Consultant and Trainer she assists others in finding their Peace with Him. She is available to provide workshops/retreats in the areas of Prayer, Discovering Your Spiritual Gifts, Christian Conflict Resolution, Anger Management, Anti-Bullying, Forgiveness, Communication Skills, Sexual Harassment Prevention, Leadership Development and Cultural Diversity. She is an experienced Mediator and has conducted trainings in the area of Conflict Resolution and Mediation.

Apostle Candace Ford is an author, a speaker and a spiritual midwife and she believes in having multiple streams of income. She is a licensed and ordained minister, the founder and visionary of Women's Impact Network, the author of the Committed 2 Commune – a 52-week devotional for women, and Co-Founder of

Love Clones, Inc. – a full branding and marketing firm for small businesses, churches and non-profit organizations. She and her husband, Kevin Ford are the apostolic overseers of Prayer Tower Ministries International.

Minister Kathy Hodge-Davis is a wife and mother. She has been in ministry since 2003. She currently serves as Youth Minister at Bethany Baptist Church in Syracuse, NY. Minister Kathy is Founder and Visionary of S.W.A.A. blog ministry.

Tracey Massey is a woman that has a gift of encouragement, a passion for renewing the mind, and a burden to see God's people live an abundant and victorious life. Through her struggles with grief, identity, self-worth, Tracey has learned that quitting is not an option. Tracey is a Certified Life Breakthrough Coach and a student at Liberty University studying Psychology and Christian Counseling. She is also the visionary and founder of EmPOWERed Life Coaching & Counseling.

Erin Mitchell is a Chicago, IL native. She accepted Jesus Christ as her Lord and Savior in 1999. After receiving Christ, her journey to fulfilling purpose and destiny began. Throughout Erin's life experiences, she has seen the power and faithfulness of God, being personally healed of a life threatening disease. Knowing God as her personal healer, she desires to assist others in experiencing the healing power of the Lord, physically, spiritually and mentally. Erin is a young adult leader at Cornerstone Christian Center in South Chicago Heights, IL and is the founder and president of A Light in a Dark Place Ministry.

Shakia Mosley is a Christian coach, author, and entrepreneur. She has a Bachelors degree in Christian Ministry. Her mission in life is to teach women how to transform from the way of the world to the way of the Word. Transitioning is often frightening for some women; however, God has called each of His daughters to a life complete in Him. She believes in order to truly understand God; we must spend time in His word. We have to cultivate a longing for the things of Him. An intimate relationship with the Father will determine your victory in life.

Trinisa Pitts is a native of Syracuse NY. Her favorite past-time is reading. She is a self-motivated individual that loves to inspire others. Her ultimate goal is to show all women that even through your wildest mess GOD can and will bring out the best. You are your Strongest Inspiration.

Anika Reese is a woman with the heart of a servant of God and His Word. She knows the importance of serving others before you can lead. A mother of four children, she considers her "Gifts from God!" She is the founder of a ministry near and dear to her heart… Restoring Beauty from Ashes. This ministry is a reflection of her life. She believes herself to be a survivor, a conqueror, a testimony. She will reach out to others that the world has disregarded and have devalued their worth, as she helps them to not only uncover, but then to restore their beauty and worth!

Sara Robillard is a New England native, currently lives in central Florida where she works full time as a preschool teacher. Writing has always been her passion. She serves as the secretary for her local chapter of American Christian Writers. Because music is a constant source of inspiration, she also aspires to be a Christian songwriter. Sara has been active in recovery programs, and is involved in the nationwide recovery ministry known as Celebrate Recovery where she functions as a leader and writes blogs for their blog on the church's website.

Daphne Tarango is a woman whose heart is for recovery—not only for her own but also for other women on their recovery journeys. She walks alongside women, comforting them with the comfort she has received from God and inspiring them to take Biblical steps to personal growth and freedom. Daphne's desire is for all who come into her life to feel the warmth of God and to know they are safe around her. Daphne's inspirational articles have appeared in Comfort Café, Inspired Women Magazine, Rest Ministries, and Mentoring Moments for Christian Women. Daphne not only writes; she also speaks at recovery events. She is a leader in a 12-step, Christ-centered recovery program at her church, where she facilitates open-share and step study groups.

Stacey Virgo is a Caribbean native, residing in Orlando, FL. She is a professional business manager, author, event specialist and a daughter of a King. A passion for the things of God, Stacey has an influence on speaking about the way we show love and compassion to others. She is the CEO and Founder of Christian Women United in Business and The Courageous Woman, a pioneering organization which unites Christian business women in sharing, uplifting, edifying, encouraging and networking using the principles of the bible. She is the owner of SHARGO USA which is professional business support company niche in the area of ministry support and event planning.

Sylvia White is a woman of faith, accepting Jesus Christ as her personal Savior in 1977. Mrs. White holds to her credit over 34 years of experience in the field of Early Childhood Education. She is also a qualified trainer at The Center for Child Care Career Development. With her ministry focus on the future leaders of this world, Mrs. White and her husband Jerry are the directors of "Extreme Children's Ministry"; an electrifying ministry for children ages 5-12. Author of "The First Year Teacher" and "The Heart of Faithfulness", Sylvia also adds to her repertoire numerous short children's stories, pre-school curriculum and is presently the director of the New Life Christian Academy of Goose Creek, SC.